Pra
"Leave the

"*Move over Tim Ferriss, there's a refreshed approach to unshackling yourself from the grueling busy-work of the grind.*

Having taken many steps to minimize the impact of wasted time, I came ready to hear what your approach would be. I found the basis in mental energy to be right on target--the minute anyone puts themselves in a position to want change, the first challenge is always overcoming their own psycho- logical barriers. Affirmations tied to habits tied to goals... you've covered critical ground to make positive change. Once I made it through, I found myself itching to do the actions. I couldn't wait to hit the street!"

Matthew Hart - *Author* and CTO Arise Virtual Solutions

"*Leave the Grind Behind is an exceptional, actionable, and unique look at how to successfully quit your day job and follow your passions. It will prime you for repeated success while also maintaining a balanced life.*

I've been able to personally see Justin Gesso's plan in action and the fantastic results it has yielded. If you're ready to quit your day job, make more money, follow your passions, and be in control of your time, I enthusiastically recommend this book for you."

Elena Pezzini, PhD - #1 Bestselling Author and Certified Life & Financial Coach – youhavegotthepower.com

"Leave the Grind Behind dives deep into the tactical steps and actions you need to start taking today to find yourself making money on your own quickly. Having left my corporate job to run a successful business of my own, I will tell you...take this model and execute on it."

Ashok Reddy - Founder and CEO, BETSOL—betsol.com

"Justin Gesso maps out how therapeutic practices, Dialectical Behavior Therapy, and Scripting all in the concept of mindset. If you want to leave any or all of your ineffective habits or lifestyle behind, follow the steps outlined in Leave the Grind Behind. You will be living a new fulfilling life, achieving your personal best."

Marcia J. Murphy, Ph.D - Licensed Clinical Psychologist

"This is it. Leave the Grind Behind shows you the way to repeatedly achieve success on your own terms. These are the exact practices I've used to achieve extraordinary results in multiple businesses."

Mark Ferguson - Owner of Multi-Million Dollar Real Estate Businesses – investfourmore.com

"Justin Gesso is the secret sauce behind a lot of successful people, myself included. This book is to the point and an easy read. Lots of highly actionable stuff here.

Do it! This will get you motivated and on the right path to doing something big in your life."

Ben Leybovich - Real Estate Investor and Entrepreneur—justaskbenwhy.com

Leave The Grind Behind

Rocket fuel to live life on your terms. Make more money, build your legacy, and quit your job.

JUSTIN GESSO

Copyright © 2017

by Gesso Wealth Consultants LLC

1110 38th Ave Suite 1

Greeley, CO 80634

Second Edition

Authored by Justin Gesso

Edited by Greg Helmerick

The author has made best efforts to determine the
sources of all quotes contained herein.

Table of Contents

SECTION 3: THE GRINDER'S ACTIONS

How to Get the Most Out of this Book

This book is dedicated to those ready to forge their own path, get more out of life, and burn their imprint on the world.

The pages ahead are packed with actions, habits, and tools that will enable your success and explode your results.

To help you stay on-track, I've simplified everything into the exact worksheets and trackers you'll need. Get them at:

grindbehindbook.com/tools

You'll also find 2 **free bonuses**:

1. 100 Tips to Quit Your Job this Year
2. The Grinder Master's Course

Introduction

My story started like most others—maybe like yours. I went to college, landed a good job, and began working my way up.

I was working *hard* at my job. I was good at it and was making what I thought was decent money. But it was stressful. It was cutting into my personal life, and I could sense myself falling out of balance.

This stress caused something inside of me to break and I ended up in the hospital—despite eating well, exercising, and being healthy (or so I thought). This stress-induced episode was truly a transformative moment for me. It was a wake-up call. I became acutely aware of the fragility of life and how limited our time is.

This event led me to re-evaluate how I was living. I consumed anything and everything in the self-improvement, success, and personal development arenas. I knew life was fleeting, and I knew there was a better way to live it.

Using the wealth of information consolidated in this book, I was able to design a life that was vastly more successful and balanced.

I made money in much more enjoyable ways. And, I made a lot more of it. Better yet, I found more time for my family, passions, and hobbies. As a result, I'm healthier, happier, and richer.

My success has not been a one-time event. Rather, I am involved in numerous successful multi-million dollar startups and product launches that consistently deliver exceptional results.

I continue to refine and analyze how I've been able to realize these achievements. To do so, I partner with a list of high-level mentors and coaches, each of whom has their hand in this book.

My goal is to bring all of these principles and teachings to you. They have catapulted and transformed my life, and they will do the same for you.

Leave the Grind Behind is about achieving greatness in life—however you define it. This book will show you how to look inside, find your driving passions, and turn those drivers into real-world results. Leave Corporate America in your rear-view mirror!

Here's the thing...I am committed to this process! I am committed to enabling *millions* to leave their job, achieve their dreams, and live a life they design.

Let's make it happen. Contact me any time at justin@grindbehindbook.com to work through this material.

Who is this Book For?

I wrote this for people who have built a good career, are probably comfortable, yet have an itch—a realization even—that *this* isn't all life is about. They wonder, *isn't there something more? Can't I do better?*

You know time is your most valuable asset. You know that spending the majority of your waking time working for someone else's dream won't let you achieve your dream life.

But through a whirlwind of events, you've ended up a Cog in the daily grind, working for an upper-middle-class salary with no real end in sight. Your dreams are fading. But you're not ready to go out without a fight.

If this sounds like you, keep reading. You are ready for more than a job. You are ready to enter a realm that will be more rewarding, more exciting, more personal. You are ready for something that, ideally, will make you a fortune.

While I hope this allows you to completely kick your job and spend as much time as you want on projects that excite you, I realize that can be a daunting proposition. If you're not quite ready, this book will give you plenty. So here goes—this book is for you if you want to:

- Quit your day job altogether and start your own business.
- Be a rock star at the job you already have, opening your career possibilities.
- Identify your personal and professional goals, then design your life around them.
- Reduce the risk of doing something big.
- Create new revenue streams, while working your current job or not.
- Purchase investment properties.
- Complete that passion-project on the side.
- Create a book, software, or other intellectual property.
- Provide for yourself and your family without compromise.
- Enjoy freedom and the best life has to offer.
- Leave a legacy.

I hope this book convinces you to leave the grind behind and start a life in which you drive the results. A life in which you earn money via multiple channels, are in control of your time, do things you enjoy, and leave a legacy that makes you proud.

Will this Book Work for You?

There is no shortage of self-help, personal-development, and get-rich-quick books on the market. To me, that's great. My life is a journey, and I need fresh sources of inspiration and ideas to keep me motivated and challenged. I hope this book provides that for you. But I also think it can do something more.

Many books come from authors who've had one particularly large success. While I'd love to fall in that category myself, this book provides a more generally accessible path. It gives you the tools to achieve repeated excellence. And it should position you to greatly increase your odds of achieving those one-time exceptional events.

To start an excellent, scalable business, you're probably looking at a couple of years of tremendously hard work with little return and no guarantee. If you already have a solid job, a mortgage, and a family to support, you know that immediately jumping into the deep end is just too risky.

But, that doesn't need to stop you. This book is a guide to transitioning from being a Cog to being a Grinder as quickly as possible while also greatly reducing your risk.

To analogize, many get-rich-quick authors have hit a one-time bases-loaded home run. And they're excited...I'd be too. They want to teach you how to step up to the plate for the first time and nail a bases-loaded home run.

I consider strong W2 wage earners as hitters of singles. Is it best to go directly from hitting singles to trying to hit a bases-loaded home run? It sounds good, but it won't be practical for everyone. Many of us would end up hitting into a triple play. And that's the danger—since it's not practical, you end up striking out. Or worse, taking no action at all.

But what if there's a better option? What if you could start hitting doubles and triples over the course of this next year? What if within two years you found yourself hitting with the bases-loaded?

That's where I will take you with this book. I will help you build the legacy you always envisioned. You will develop a plan for leaving the grind behind, execute on it, and do so with minimal risk.

What Have this Book's Principles Done for Me?

Quite simply, this book's principles have allowed me to say, *I will never go back.* I've made it to the other side, and the grass is greener.

These principles allowed me to "break out" from the standard day-job mentality. This is a very scary proposition for many; it was for me too.

I provided the sole income for my wife and small child. I was already making good money. I was comfortable. I was stable. I had been conditioned early to work hard at school, go to college, keep going to school, grind it out 9-5…or in reality, 7-5+. I just needed to keep working my way up the corporate ladder, then…

And what's the conditioning we receive for starting our own business? Heck, everyone tells you that startup businesses fail all the time. Not only that, but you can't do it unless you have massive amounts of money and time.

So I had a ton to risk! And I had a lifetime of beliefs to overcome. But, I practiced the principles in this book and quickly realized that I had it all wrong. In fact, the risk of staying in the grind was *massively* greater than the risk of leaving it behind.

That's right: the standard view of risk is completely backward. Indeed, once I left the grind behind, I immediately started making much more money than I did in my "good" six-figure job. I was hitting doubles and triples. I was back in control of the one asset that is truly limited—my time. I was able to:

- 2x my 6-figure corporate income within just 1.5 years of leaving the grind.
- 2x my net worth within 2 years of leaving the grind.
- Earn 60% of my income from passive and scalable sources.
- Be ground level at several multi-million dollar startups.

All while working fewer hours and being in charge of my time. Is my journey over? No…far from it. I'm much more successful, savvy, and happy. But I feel like I'm just scratching the surface. I love the path I'm on and know there's so much more.

In fact, I'm currently involved in five highly scalable projects, all of which have the ability and scope to impact millions of people. These are bases-loaded situations. I may miss, but if any one of these projects breaks out, I will receive a windfall, propelling my success to an entirely new level. But even if this doesn't happen, I'm still covered.

Because of this, taking big swings is no longer risky for me. I've established a steady base of income from multiple sources, many of which are passive.

So while I've already achieved the success many people can only dream of, I am at the cusp of much more.

How to Use this Book

You can't follow an ordinary path and expect extraordinary results. You need to avoid the repetitive trap many of us fall into, commonly called "the grind." For many people, the grind offers comfort and stability.

I argue, though, that this comfort and stability comes at an incredible price. When you stand at your last step and look back at your life, will you have accomplished what you wanted? Will you have spent your only life well?

You should want to get the best out of life. You should be excited to wake up and accomplish greatness. You should be able to achieve a balanced life, reaching high levels of achievement in terms of money, relationships, health, community, and spirit. You should have *fun* doing it! And you should expect real results.

Leave the Grind Behind is a mix of mental techniques and practical actions. These concepts come from combining the best from the modern, ancient, and business worlds. Don't reinvent: follow the clues success leaves.

These concepts will take you from clarifying your purpose to executing on ambitious goals. This book will also show you how to apply these skills and turn your motivation into money.

Within this book, you'll find information and resources to help you prep, decide wisely, and pull the trigger yourself. You will start earning more money and living a more satisfying life.

And if you don't yet know what you want to do, this book will help you uncover that.

Last, this book will mold your thinking toward scalable money strategies, which are the key to achieving unusually large levels of success.

Personal First, Business Second

With a name like *Leave the Grind Behind*, you might be surprised to see such an emphasis on personal discovery. If you want to be successful on your own, you must love what you do. You must absorb yourself in it.

For this reason, it is critical you start by understanding yourself, your priorities, and your goals before ever building a business.

While this might sound obvious, most people do the opposite and start with work goals first. In fact, that's exactly how we end up in the grind. Maybe you took a job out of desperation. Or, you liked its pay. Your plan was to get a job and let the rest fall into place.

What if, instead, you designed your life around personal goals? Would your current job still suffice?

This book assumes you're not desperate for work. Rather, this book is for people who want more from life. They want their life—and by necessity—their work to be satisfying and fulfilling.

If you're ready to uncover your passions, identify personal goals, and then build an effective money making strategy upon that foundation, this book is for you. I'll help you find true nexus of success—where your interests and passions meet the needs of many.

What is Not in this Book

This book does *not* focus on the technical analysis of starting a new business. While I have my MBA, have managed numerous product launches, and consult regularly for multi-million dollar startups, I am not here to present you with an A-Z list of due-diligence steps.

Rather than finding reasons to poke holes in business ideas, the focus of this book is on *why* you would want to pursue your passions.

The *why* is the fuel that will ignite your desire to work on the details that help you break out on your own. The practices in this book give you reasons to leave the grind behind...rather than reasons *not* to.

There are always risks, and you can easily focus too heavily on them. While other books may approach entrepreneurship with analytical frameworks, I find that most people get paralyzed by analysis and focus too much on the negatives. As a result, they *never take action.*

This book will provide you the tools to greatly minimize risk, but will do so in a unique manner that will keep you moving forward.

The reality is that there are countless opportunities out there. It's time to take yours. Don't let someone else. If you try to account for everything up front, you'll find you never swing the bat.

Why the Focus on Mental Practices?

Looking at the Table of Contents, you'll see the entire first section is about mental practices.

These practices make up the critical foundation of your success. If you want to leave the grind behind, you must have mental clarity and focus. You need motivation. You need enthusiasm. You need all cylinders firing.

Many people I have talked to throughout my journey tell me they *want* to leave the grind behind. They envy those who have. They are not short on smarts. They do very well for their companies. So what's stopping them?

The answer is mindset. They misunderstand the risks. They see becoming a Grinder (more on that term later) as a fantasy—not something regular people do.

Mindset is cultivated in Section 1 of this book. If you want to become a Grinder, don't underestimate the mindset portion of this book.

I'm far from alone in my approach to working your mind first. The practices in this book are used by NASA, US Olympic teams, doctors, the $100B US advertising industry, and *literally all* of the massively successful people I know.

In fact, Thomas C. Corley conducted a five-year study of self-made millionaires which concluded, *"Thinking is the key to their [self-made millionaires] success."* Specifically, the study found these subjects typically dedicate 15-30 minutes each day to focusing their mental energy deeply and personally on their success. Exactly as I'll prescribe here.

A word of caution though: other books and programs push the seductive idea that all you need to do is imagine your future and it will happen. While deliberate thinking is vastly important, it is not sufficient on its own.

On top of having clarity, purpose, and focus, you also need to take corresponding action. This book gives you the tools to create a mental edge, but it also gives you the tools to take successful, tactical, and habitual actions. When these factors are combined, you will literally have no choice but to achieve your own greatness.

The mind is what matters. The mind is what separates. The mind is it. Within this book, you'll learn how to have the type of mind that can fuel you to leave the grind behind.

Is Wanting a Lot of Money Bad?

I'll assume, since you've picked up this book, that you want more money. Hopefully you not only want some money; you want a *lot* of money. That's great.

Throughout this book, you'll learn ways to "plant the seed" of businesses that can grow and scale, with the goal of earning you a lot of money.

But making a lot of money carries a stigma. So, is wanting a lot of money bad?

Let me answer first by saying you likely want to leave the grind behind for more reasons than money alone. Personally, I wanted more time with my family and hobbies, and I wanted to work on my passions and goals—not someone else's. I wanted to be in control of my time and build my future. But I couldn't do that without money.

Fundamentally, we should all want a lot of money. When you make a massive amount of money, you're not taking from anyone else. Rather, you are receiving validation that you've added value to a massive number of people.

You're gaining the ability to control your time and be in charge of your life. You're gaining the ability to donate copious amounts to charity, if you want. You're gaining the ability to have choices.

If you feel guilty about pursuing money, get over it right now. Money gives you time and flexibility, and those are beautiful things. Money in and of itself is not bad.

If you have mental baggage about this topic, you will struggle with being successful. Pay attention to Section 1 of this book and alter those beliefs ASAP.

Grinder Actions

To bridge the gap between education and execution, you will find Grinder Actions at the end of each chapter. These actions are designed to fuel your excitement, tune you to your goals, and help you put rubber to pavement.

The actions are structured in a sequential manner, with each building upon the last.

Grinder Habits

"You will never change your life until you change something you do daily. The secret of your success is found in your daily routine."

~ Darren Hardy, The Compound Effect ~

In addition to Grinder Actions, you will add numerous habits to your daily routine. These habits are vital to going from where you are today to where you want to be. They should become deeply ingrained in your routine.

Don't worry: these habits will not dominate your day. They are designed as efficient ways to engage your mind and drive true change in your life.

Habits form what Darren Hardy has termed the "Compound Effect." Exactly in the way compound interest works wonders with money, habits compound to work wonders in your life.

It's the small daily choices that add up to deliver big results.

Put the *Grinder Habits* into play, give them time, and be amazed at what they deliver in your life.

> "The individual who wants to reach the top in business must appreciate the might and force of habit. He must be quick to break those habits that can break him—and hasten to adopt those practices that will become the habits that help him achieve the success he desires."
>
> ~ J. Paul Getty ~

How this Book is Structured

Leave the Grind Behind is divided into three distinct sections. First, you will learn how to marshal your internal resources toward taking massive action—*Grinder Mindset*.

Second, you will learn the secret sauce to minimizing risk and leap-frogging results, which is to have and effectively manage the right people network—*Grinder Network*.

Third, I'll dive into the initial steps you can take to earn money and live a better life as Grinder—*Grinder Action*.

The Grinder Success Map

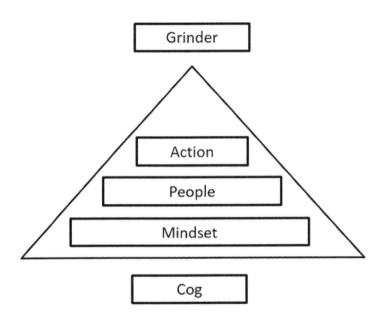

Final Prep before You Start

In order to get the most out of these actions and habits, you will need to buy a notebook or journal that you can dedicate to leaving the grind behind.

Second, you'll want to buy a stack of blank notecards. Several habits require you to utilize notecards for easy review on the go.

Third, head over to **grindbehindbook.com/tools** and grab the downloads, including the worksheets and daily trackers. They will help you more easily organize your habits and actions.

And last, I recommend buying a high-quality pen that you use only for the activities described in this book. Having a special implement dedicated to changing your life is incredibly powerful.

CHAPTER 1

Cogs vs Grinders

Before Section 1 kicks off, some terminology will ensure we're on the same page.

The word "grind" carries a lot of positive and negative connotations. It's a great, emotional word. The trick is being on the right side of its definition.

Cogs

If you're "in the grind," that means you're spending Monday through Friday, 8-5 (or more), working for *someone else's* dreams, passions, and riches. Your grinding realizes someone else's vision. Your grinding makes millions for someone else. You are a Cog.

Cogs grind away day-after-day, and the term "grind" means monotony. It means your life is a blur. The weekend is over, back to *the grind*.

Cog life revolves around external benefits. While you get compensated for what you're doing, it's not enough. Even if you earn a solid six-figure salary, have a nice house, and are contributing to your 401K, grinding for someone else can leave you feeling empty.

And I assume that's why you're reading this book. You're a Cog. You might be a highly successful Cog. I hope so. You might be offended I'm calling you a Cog, but you know it's true.

I've talked to many successful Cogs who have done everything right. They studied hard and graduated with strong degrees. They entered a corporate job, bled for their company, and climbed the ladder into leadership positions. But once there, they realize life is moving fast and they want more. They want something they'll never achieve as a Cog.

Grinders

So what's the positive definition of "grind?" "Grinder," of course. Don't confuse "the grind" I'm telling you to ditch with "the Grinder" I want you to become.

Being a Grinder means you grind hard for *your* personal purpose and goals, not for someone else's. To leave the grind behind, make no mistake, you need to *grind.* You need to grind hard. You're just doing it for yourself, and let me tell you—you'll love it.

As a Grinder, you spend your one, short life building *your* legacy and *your* unique imprint on this world.

Average people cannot accomplish these things, but that's because average people fold under the pressure. Average people find all of the reasons not to become a Grinder. Average people cannot commit to big endeavors. Grinders can. This book will show you how to be a Grinder.

Grinder
Summary

Here's a table that summarizes the information in this chapter and helps you quickly determine if you're a Cog or a Grinder. Almost everyone is a Cog, but you're taking steps to change your standard conditioning and behavior. Over time, you should see more and more of the Grinder principles applying to your life.

Cog	Grinder
Stuck in the grind	Left the grind behind
Builds someone else's vision	Builds own vision
Earns limited wages	Scalable and passive earnings
Builds someone else's wealth	Builds own wealth
Time is controlled by someone else	Time is greatest resource and is self-controlled
Leaves limited legacy	Leaves massive legacy

Grinder Action:
Baseline Yourself

Before you dive head-first into the material in this book, it's a good idea to understand where you actually fall on the Cog-Grinder continuum.

This two-minute quiz is designed to give you an idea of where you are today. It will also trigger some introspection and ideally give you some strong motivation to blast through this book and apply its principles to your life.

While you can take the quiz here, I recommend you head over to **grindbehindbook.com/quiz**. You will receive immediate feedback and see how you place compared to others.

1. How do you earn money?

- I work for someone else at a full-time W2 (standard) job with no substantial additional income sources.
- I earn the majority my income from non-W2 work, but
- I believe I can still earn more.

2. This is how I approach success:

- I do not have a daily practice for focusing on achieving the life I want.
- I have goals and work toward them, but don't really have a consistent routine I follow.
- I have a daily routine of practices that helps me clarify the life I want and focus on achieving it. I'm always looking for better and more efficient routines.

3. Which factor below will contribute most to your success?

- My education
- My work experience
- The money I have right now
- My people network

4. This is how I feel about my work:

- I'm not personally invested in my work. I work for the money, which may not be enough.
- I enjoy my work, but if it wasn't my job, I wouldn't do it.
- I obsess passionately over it. In fact, it doesn't feel like work.

5. Which answer best describes how you're spending your one, short life?

- I don't have goals.
- I'm working hard on goals...but they are mostly someone else's (my boss' or company's). If push comes to shove, I set aside personal goals for goals I can't choose.
- I'm working hard on MY goals. MY goals take priority.

6. The following best describes my personal income:

- I have one source of income.
- I have multiple sources of significant income.
- I have multiple sources of significant income, some of which are passive (rentals, royalties, etc...).
- I have multiple sources of significant income, some of which are passive and some of which are scalable (can grow massively).

7. Do you have a mentor, coach, or mastermind group you meet with regularly?

- No
- Yes

8. I BELIEVE I can have the life I want while also making unusually large amounts of money.

- No, in order to earn a lot of money, I have to give up time for myself, family, vacations, and more. To reach unusual success, I have to sacrifice everything else.
- No, you have to be lucky to make unusual amounts of money--it's not related to how I spend my time.
- No, just no.
- Yes

9. This is what I think about time:

- I never have enough time in the day. With my regular job, I don't see how I could ever start something big and leave the grind behind.
- Time is a blur. I'm not substantially different than I was last year. It's amazing how time flies.
- Time is the only real limited asset. Money is not limited. Money buys time. Time is what I want to manage. If I manage it, I can have plenty of it to achieve whatever I want.

10. This is what I want from life:

- I want to be comfortable. I want a solid, steady job. I want to be middle or upper-middle class. Health benefits and consistency are important to me. I am fine working all week and having the weekends left for my time.
- I want everything. I want to achieve my dreams. I want a lot of money and time. I want to pursue my interests. I want to leave a legacy. I want to make an impact on the world. I want to be exceptional and achieve unusually outstanding results.

11. I know how to maximize my brainpower:

- No
- Yes. I have methods built in to my daily routine to optimize my brain and focus it on achieving my goals. I understand how the subconscious works and employ it daily to my advantage.

Quiz Scoring

The best answers are in the table below. For each Grinder Answer, give yourself 10 points. Once complete, jot down your total points.

The total is your baseline. The higher the score, the more Grinder-oriented you are. The lower the score, the more room for improvement you have. You should take this quiz regularly to see how your score changes.

Don't worry: I don't expect you to answer these as a Grinder would. This is a journey, and your answers will evolve over time.

Question	Grinder Answer
1. How do you earn your money?	I earn the majority of my income from non-W2 work, but I believe I can still earn more.
2. This is how I approach success:	I have a daily routine of practices that helps me clarify the life I want and focus on achieving it. I'm always looking for more efficient routines.
3. Which factor below will contribute most to your success?	My people network
4. This is how I feel about my work:	I obsess passionately over it. In fact, it doesn't feel like work.
5. How are you spending your one short life?	I'm working hard on MY goals. MY goals take priority.
6. The following best describes my personal income:	I have multiple sources of significant income, some of which are passive and some of which are scalable (can grow massively).

Question	Grinder Answer
7. Do you have a mentor, coach, or Mastermind Group you meet with regularly?	Yes
8. I BELIEVE I can have the life I want while also making unusually large amounts of money.	Yes
9. This is what I think about time:	Time is the only real limited asset. Money is not limited. Money buys time. Time is what I want to manage. If I manage it, I can have plenty of it to achieve whatever I want.
10. This is what I want from life:	I want everything. I want to achieve my dreams. I want a lot of money and time. I want to pursue my interests. I want to leave a legacy. I want to make an impact on the world. I want to be exceptional and achieve unusually outstanding results.

Grinder Habit:
Measure Quarterly

Most Grinder Habits will be completed on a daily basis, but this chapter's habit is different. You should get in the habit of assessing your life on a regular basis to ensure you are progressing accordingly.

In the upcoming chapters, you will learn plenty about setting goals and reviewing your progress. But it is also important to do a broader baseline review of your life using a consistent measurement system.

This means you should go to **grindbehindbook.com/quiz** and complete the quiz once per quarter. Write down your results and track the changes over time.

SECTION 1

The Grinder
Mindset

SECTION 1 INTRODUCTION:

The Grinder's Mind

This section will be a surprise to many of the readers of this book. You will not find content like this in a traditional MBA program or entrepreneurship course. What you will find here is the critical foundation for leaving the grind behind.

It is the ingredient most of us miss in our standard upbringing and education. It's what Grinders know and Cogs don't.

And face it, you probably already have better circumstances than many others who have already left the grind behind. So why them and not you? Mindset.

This section provides a framework designed to drive unparalleled focus, motivation, and mental acuity.

While you may approach this with skepticism, I urge you to put its actions and habits to practice and commit to them for at least two months. The daily habits are simple and will not require much of your valuable time.

If after two months, you're not shocked by the changes you experience in your life, I'll eat my hat.

Your energy and excitement will become palpable. Your attitude will become contagious and infectious. You will be ready to explode, leaving your mark on the world.

After all, you can read all of the practical advice in the world, but unless you have the mindset to take action, you'll never become a Grinder. So get ready to work on the way you process the world.

CHAPTER 2

The Grinder Attitude

"Keep your thoughts positive because your thoughts become your words. Keep your words positive because your words become your behavior. Keep your behavior positive because your behavior becomes your habits. Keep your habits positive because your habits become your values. Keep your values positive because your values become your destiny."

~ Mahatma Gandhi ~

Significant change in your life begins with attitude. In this chapter, you will learn how attitude can affect your success and how you can go about adjusting it.

Let me be clear, if your attitude isn't right, you'll never leave the grind behind. It's that simple.

Why is this? Let's explore…

Negative people see problems.

Positive people see opportunities to add value.

Negative people complain about their circumstances, people, the economy, the government, their boss, and more.

Positive people take ownership for their situation and find ways to change their circumstances if needed.

Do those negative characteristics sound compatible with Grinder life? No. You need a positive attitude. And in fact, in order to leave the grind behind, you need an unbelievably, exceptionally, ridiculously positive attitude.

Grinders run into hurdles, nay-sayers, self-doubt, closed doors, failure, failure, and more failure. Most people cannot push through this degree of adversity.

But guess what: with the right attitude, pushing through is not actually that hard. In fact, if you can stick through the initial resistance, you'll find yourself in a small percentage of the population—somewhere *most* people won't go. Somewhere Cogs won't go. You cross the line in the sand and become a Grinder, because you pushed through instead of turning back.

And the exact reason you'll see better results than *most* people is because you went somewhere that most people won't go...all thanks to your attitude.

I hope that you already have an excellent, positive attitude. This chapter outlines just what I mean by "positive attitude." It will also give you some tools to push your attitude to the next level.

Even better, as you'll see, having a positive attitude will also help improve your personal life, including your health, your relationships, your money, and much more.

> "All day long, you are selectively paying attention to something, and much more often than you may suspect, you can take charge of this process to good effect. Indeed, your ability to focus on this and suppress that is the key to controlling your experience and, ultimately, your well-being."
>
> ~ Winifred Gallagher, Rapt ~

Negative Attitude for Cog Results

Do you think people with negative attitudes can do something big? Can they quit the grind and start businesses? Can they enjoy a balanced life? There are certainly exceptions out there, but I think you'll be hard-pressed to find negative people who are successful across multiple areas of life.

Consider these statements:

- No one will ever buy my product
- My customers are all idiots
- My idea probably won't work
- My family won't support me
- I'll never have enough money, time, or energy to do this
- I won't really make any money from it anyway
- I'll have to deal with all sorts of legal trouble
- I'll probably have to beg my boss for my job back

If you say any of these things, they'll probably come true. This is precisely why negative people are so comfortable being bat-on-their-shoulder Cogs, while positive people swing for the fences.

Positive Attitude for Grinder Results

Self-made millionaire, Steve Siebold, has interviewed over 1,200 of the world's wealthiest people. His findings are summarized in this simple statement: *"When the rich need money, they don't wonder if it's possible, they simply begin creating new ideas that solve problems. They don't waste mental energy worrying or wondering about their ability to produce cash[,] they direct their concentration towards creative thinking."*

In other words, rather than focusing on the challenges and negative possibilities, Grinders focus on the positive side of the equation: creation. Let me drive the point home a bit more with a real-life experiment I observed.

In a past Cog job of mine, over the course of 5+ years, I was in a unique position to observe just over 500 people who were in very similar circumstances. Despite these circumstantial similarities, the difference in life results was astonishing.

These people were in unionized jobs. They had the exact same income, the exact same job, and shared many other identical factors in their personal lives. Despite this, I saw incredibly different outcomes in all aspects of their lives: health, wealth, friends, job success, personal success, and overall life satisfaction.

Why do people in similar circumstances have such different outcomes?

While I'm not going to present empirical data on my findings, I do want to attach some validity to my observations. When I

LEAVE THE GRIND BEHIND

earned my MBA, my focus was on statistics, which gave me great knowledge of how to isolate variables and identify causality.

Further, my profession at the time was focused on Six Sigma, which had me putting statistical analysis to practice every day.

> "...a rare convergence of insights from both neuroscience and psychology suggests a paradigm shift in how to think about this cranial laser and its role in behavior: thoughts, feelings, and actions. Like fingers pointing to the moon, other diverse disciplines from anthropology to education, behavioral economics to family counseling, similarly suggest that the skillful management of attention is the sine qua non of the good life and the key to improving virtually every aspect of your experience, from mood to productivity to relationships."
>
> ~ Gallagher, Winifred, Behavioral Scientist. Rapt ~

The living laboratory—how I was able to watch the positivity theory unfold

My lab:

- Large sample size of 500 people
- 5 years of observation
- Same professional circumstances and expectations
- Same paySimilar professional backgrounds, skillsets, and interests
- Similar home neighborhoods
- Similar age groups

This was a generally open and talkative group of employees. People told me about their life circumstances. I constantly overheard discussions about personal and professional issues. There was no shortage of information to go by. And based on the information at hand, some very obvious trends bubbled to the top.

> "The greatest discovery of all time is that a person can change his future by merely changing his attitude."
>
> ~ Oprah Winfrey ~

Same circumstances, different outcomes

As I watched these people, I found they generally fell into 3 groups containing the following characteristics:

Group 1 - The Positive People (bats swinging)

- High work performance
- Good personal financial situation
- Positive personal lifeGood health
- Resilience and adaptability to change
- Generally socialized and found social status by discussing things they were doing in the *future* or the activities and hobbies they had

Group 2 - The Negative People (bats on shoulders)

- Poor work performance
- Poor personal financial situation (generally in debt)

- Negative personal life
- Poor health
- Poor resilience (the *old days* were always better)
- Resistant to change
- Generally socialized and found social status by *complaining and gossiping*

Group 3 - The Rest (hitting singles)

- There was a third, very small group. Less than 10% did not share many details about their life.
- They arrived, sat down, did their job, and left.

Remember, these people all had nearly identical work circumstances and experienced similar circumstances outside of work. Could there have been other factors at play apart from outlook on life? Of course.

I tried slicing and dicing by age, gender, marital status, and just about any other defining characteristic I could find. But after years of observation, it was beyond obvious to me: having a *positive outlook* was the number one factor at play.

Attitude played a very key role with money too. Negative people regularly had money problems (even though they were well payed). Here is what the negative group did:

- Talked about debt
- Complained that raises were too small
- Griped about taxes

The positive people, on the other hand, often had very nice things. They generally had beautiful houses and cars. And they weren't in debt. Many were saving for their children's future. Here's what the positive group did:

- Talked about savings and investments
- Discussed future plans
- Controlled their situation

Where did I fall on this money spectrum? When I was making the same amount of money these people were, I felt *rich*! I couldn't believe it. When I was making about 2/3 of what they were making, I felt rich too. Back when I was even younger, my girlfriend (and now wife) was making about half of what they were making, and I thought she was rich. And so did she! We were positive about the money in our lives. We were happy for what we had and our financial results were and continue to be phenomenal.

What was the real take away from this living lab?

Here's the real "ah-ha" from all of this: having a positive attitude *causes* positive results. Said another way: rather than being happy because you have a successful life, you are successful because you have a happy life.

This is a powerful concept. Please pause and make sure you understand it: *by focusing on your attitude first, results follow.*

> "Thanks to this cutting-edge science, we now know that happiness is the precursor to success, not merely the result."
>
> ~ Shawn Achor, MA, The Happiness Advantage ~

In my living lab, positive people were constantly seeing the good in life and they were being rewarded for it by having more positive things to enjoy. The negative people, on the other hand, constantly had new things to complain about.

I had always assumed people grew salty and crabby because bad things happened to them. And I assumed happy people had been given many things to celebrate in life, which is why they were happy. But my experiment showed otherwise.

As I began looking into this, it turns out there is a ton of research on the topic. If you're interested in learning more and gaining insight from actual experiments, I highly recommend starting with *The Happiness Advantage* by Shawn Achor.

The more research I did, the more questions I had. Why did having a positive attitude seem to drive positive results? Why wasn't it the other way around? Why hadn't I learned about this in school? How can I apply this with 100% vigor in my own life?

In terms of what is causing this, the underlying answer is straightforward. This is a matter of noticing what you're thinking about. All around you right now, many, many things are happening.

If you weren't able to focus, your mind would be completely overloaded. But because you can focus, you're able to shut out the unimportant and observe what is important—as defined by you.

This is why, when you begin shopping for a specific new car, you start seeing it everywhere. You are telling your brain what to see.

Here's the good news: you can apply this principle more broadly and tell your brain to see the positive in the world. And this positive lens you apply to the world has far-reaching consequences.

Winifred Gallagher brought findings from numerous scientific studies, spanning neuroscience to psychology, into her award- winning book Rapt. In referencing a set of such studies, she elaborates on this phenomenon as follows:

"These inventive experiments on emotion's effects on attention confirm something that you've often experienced.... When you feel frightened, angry, or sad, reality contracts until whatever is upsetting you takes up the whole world— at least the one between your ears. Life seems like a vale of tears, the future looks bleak, and the only memories that come to mind are unpleasant. The best explanation for why bad feelings shrink your focus is that in a potentially ominous situation, homing in on and reacting to any trouble quickly is more important than taking your time to get the big picture.

Just as bad feelings constrict your attention so you can focus on dealing with danger or loss, good feelings widen it, so you can expand into new territory— not just regarding your visual field, but also your mind-set. This broader, more generous cognitive context helps you to think more flexibly and creatively and to take in a situation's larger implications. Offering an example, Fredrickson says that when you feel upbeat, you're much likelier to recognize a near-stranger of another race— something that most people usually fail to do. 'Good feelings widen the lens through which you see the world,' she says. 'You think more in terms of relationship and connect more dots. That sense of oneness helps you feel in harmony, whether with nature, your family, or your neighborhood.'" - Gallagher, Winifred (2009-03-09). Rapt: Attention and the Focused Life.

How Does a Grinder Attitude Work in Practice?

Here's how you—as a Grinder—can leverage a positive attitude to drive real-world results:

1. Positive people see opportunity

If you have a positive outlook about achieving something, you simply don't let little distractions and speed bumps get in the way. You stay focused on your goal. If path A doesn't work, you divert to path B.

And if you see other people are having trouble with something, it's not a problem—it's an opportunity. Perhaps it's something to fix while earning the chance to improve lives.

As a positive person, you see reasons to achieve your goals. Negative people see problems and stop; they get stuck as a Cog. Negative people focus on past complications and past issues. It's hard to plan for the future if you're stuck in the past. Positive people look to the future. Grinders see a future of opportunity.

2. Positive people happen to life

Life happens to negative people. Negative people are victims. Things are always happening *to* them. They are not in control. How can you achieve what you want if you don't think you're in control? You can't, so you suck it up and remain Cogged down.

Positive people are in control. They are the drivers. They take responsibility. If they don't like their situation, they change it. Life doesn't happen to them. They happen to life. They become a Grinder and change the world.

With this sort of attitude, it's much easier to accept and adopt change. Negative attitudes breed rigidity. Feeling in control of the world makes you much more open and excited about change. You feel the world is flexibly and malleable; therefore, you adapt quickly and without trouble.

Indeed, a 1995 Menninger Institute of New York study determined the most important quality for business success is flexibility—the ability to adapt change. Keep a positive mind, and stay valuable.

3. Positive people attract other positive people

Positivity drives synergy. Having other positive people in your life increases opportunities. Hang out with Grinders long enough, and you can't help but become one yourself.

Maybe your positive circle of friends recommends a great investment. Maybe they have a great business venture or recommend a life-changing book. Being around positive people fuels your own attitude and results.

If you hang around with a bunch of negative Cogs, what do your conversations look like? The president sucks. Work sucks. The weather sucks. My drive to work in the weather sucked. My coworkers suck. My boss sucks. Do these sound like thoughts that will lead to becoming a Grinder?

4. Positive people have programmed themselves to extract the positive from life

As touched on earlier, no one can notice everything in life. Look at the thousands and thousands of things that surround you right now. You cannot possibly absorb and reflect on everything you walk past. Two people can look at the exact same room and notice completely different things.

Wouldn't you prefer to notice the positive? Positive people do. And you know what? When you notice positive things, you feel great, which gets you even more in tune with noticing the positive things life has to offer.

As a Grinder, you find the excellent things in life that can provide value to others. You cannot have or sell a great idea without first having a spark of positive creativity. You see something great and cannot wait to share it. What problem are you going to solve for the world? What opportunity do you see?

> "Positive emotions loosen up people's thought patterns, leading them to think more broadly and expansively, making unusual connections between ideas."
>
> ~Teresa Amabile, Ph.D. ~

Can You Learn to be Positive?

What if you're negative today? You can absolutely learn to be positive. That's a big part of what this book will help you do.

If you're negative, the single biggest hurdle will be acknowledging you are negative and admitting you need to change. If you can do that, you're on your way. This book is a great resource to get you started.

What if you have you had many bad things happen to you? Most people have. Some have experienced far worse things than others. In fact, even if you've had something terrible happen to you, I bet there is someone who has had something far worse and would say it became the pivotal moment in their life, causing them to make a quantum leap forward.

I don't mean to discount bad events in people's lives, but bad events can define you in very different ways. Don't see these as stumbling blocks. Reflect and grieve appropriately, but then move forward and find the positive in life as a whole.

If you're already positive, you can do better. I promise! I surround myself with positive people, books, and circumstances. I stepped onto the positive spiral ride. It's fun. I love it. I see results. I have one life to live, and I'm going to make sure I get everything out of it I want.

Grinder Summary

1. If your attitude isn't right, you'll never leave the grind behind. It's that simple. Grinders have a rockin' attitude.
2. Positive outcomes result from having a positive attitude, not the other way around.
3. Pushing through challenges is not actually that hard. In fact, if you can stick through your initial resistance to leaving the grind behind, you'll find yourself in a small percentage of the population—somewhere most people won't go. And that's exactly why you'll see better results than most people.
4. Positive people happen to life, see opportunity, and attract
5. positive people and results.
6. Want to learn more about positivity and their relationship to life results? Read *The Happiness Advantage* by Shawn Achor.
7. Want to dive into how attitude and attention can alter your
8. life? Read *Rapt* by Winifred Gallagher.

Grinder Action: Grinder Attitude Experiment

Do the attitude experiment quickly yourself. You will come to the same conclusion as me in a matter of minutes.

Think of a person in your life who has a negative attitude. These people are easy to identify: they complain and gossip. Now think of a person who has a positive attitude. Think about these two people and their outcomes.

Write their names down on a piece of paper and then answer these questions for each.

- How is their health?
- Do they like their job and coworkers?
- What's their home and personal life like?
- Are they in debt or have savings?
- Are they generous and giving?
- Do they get good service or bad service at restaurants?
- Are they lucky?
- Do they get raises at work? Bonuses?
- Are they learners?
- What sort of people and circumstances surround them?
- What's their general mood?
- Will they look back at their life and feel like they lived it to their fullest?
- Are they a leader?
- Could they leave the grind behind?
- Are they a Cog or a Grinder?

Now, write down your name. Answer these same questions for yourself? How does your attitude rate relative to the people you chose?

Grinder Habit:
Positive Memory and Expectations

A very powerful habit that helps drive positivity is simple to do and quite fun. This habit should be done nightly before bed to ensure you go to sleep happy and with great expectations for tomorrow.

The habit is designed to establish a positive memory from the day and also set a positive expectation for tomorrow. You are not focused on the "now;" rather, you are focused on the immediate past and immediate future.

- First, write down 5 things you greatly enjoyed today. What made you happy today?
- Second, write down 5 things you look forward to tomorrow. What will make you happy tomorrow?

Deliberately focusing on positive experiences helps direct what you want more of in life. Writing it down helps you internalize it on multiple levels. Tactically transferring it to a physical surface and seeing it engages other parts of your brain. Put these experiences in your journal so you can track them over time.

If you have a family, do this exercise with your spouse and kids. It will generate a stronger bond and better sense of positivity across your entire household.

CHAPTER 3

Define Your Legacy

What's your legacy? Where do you want to go? Are you maximizing life? If you leave the grind behind, where the heck will you go?

These questions are very important to ask yourself. The answers will give you long-term vision. They will give you a foundation and direction.

After all, the best businesses have purposes and missions. Shouldn't you have the same?

Answer Your Life Purpose

Now that you have that positive Grinder's attitude, the world is your oyster. You see enormous possibility. Here's your chance to define how you fit in. Here's your chance to define the impact you want to make.

Creating your own definition means you feel responsible for your life. Your results are not dependent on your circumstances; they're dependent on you.

If you accept that, you also need to accept you are responsible for determining your legacy and purpose. No one is sitting out there ready to hand over your life purpose. You choose your purpose. This is empowering.

Your life purpose will serve as the basis for how you lead your life as a Grinder. Your future goals and actions will all be aligned with your life purpose. Your behaviors, values, choices, and joy will all also work in concert with your life purpose.

> "Who am I?" "What is the purpose of my life?" These questions arise spontaneously throughout our lives, either unbidden or through conscious intent. Anyone who wishes to live an authentic life must answer these questions, regardless of whether they believe in the existence of the soul or practice a religion. If these queries remain unanswered, life will more than likely remain superficial and empty, in spite of any material abundance. If you wish to make the soul's journey, then I suggest you ask yourself these questions relentlessly and ruthlessly, and listen carefully."
>
> ~ Ilchi Lee ~

Your purpose realized is your legacy.

Successful Businesses Define Their Purpose; You Should Too

Successful business leaders know that to achieve incredible results, they had better understand the purpose of that business. Businesses that thrive, improve, and grow use tools such as mission statements and corporate visions.

These principles also apply to you as a future Grinder. If you're looking to realize incredible results from your life, shouldn't you have a well-defined purpose, too?

Benefits of Defining Your Destination

Having a big-picture and long-term view on life is a key factor to achieving big things.

Dr. Edward Banfield of Harvard performed a highly in-depth study looking into what factors allowed people to move up from one social class to another. The findings are available in his book, *The Unheavenly City*. In it, he comes to the conclusion that "time perspective" is the most important factor.

This means people who think about and set goals further in the future make bigger moves in their lives. People who don't progress think in terms of days, weeks, and months. People who make big moves think in years and decades. The sharper clarity you have on what you want in the future, the more likely you are to achieve it.

After all, which of these do you think will lead to a transformed life?

- You are going to the gym so you can lose 5 pounds by bikini season.
- You are going to the gym so you can be active and vibrant in retirement.

Having a life purpose gives you this long-term perspective.

Purpose cures boredom

"True happiness... is not attained through self-gratification, but through fidelity to a worthy purpose."

~ Helen Keller ~

If someone tells me they're bored, I am shocked. When you consider we all have one life, it is difficult to imagine not wanting to live that life to its fullest and find some way to make it as meaningful as possible to yourself and others. Why do people accept being bored Cogs so readily?

Personally, I am never bored. I have so many things I want to do, I have the opposite problem! I attribute this to having a life purpose.

Purpose keeps you from wasting time on the wrong activities

"The mystery of human existence lies not in just staying alive, but in finding something to live for."

~ Fyodor Dostoyevsky ~

Once you know where you're going in life, it's very easy to understand which activities support your life purpose and which don't. This gives you near red light/green light clarity into everything you do.

Additionally, having deep purpose helps me cope with routine tasks. We all have things we don't like about our job, household chores, or some other aspect of our lives.

Even though your life purpose will let you know which of these items you can abandon, some will have to stay. However, those routine tasks that stay become more tolerable because you can see how they fit into a bigger picture.

What's more tolerable: doing a mundane task in exchange for $12 per hour, or doing that same mundane task as a step toward realizing your life purpose?

Purpose gives you passion to wake up and do something big

"Success demands singleness of purpose."

~ Vince Lombardi ~

I like to think of my life purpose as the ultimate guide for my life. It is made up of my unique traits, my values, and my mission. From this, I am able to easily derive goals, line up actions, and make decisions quickly and confidently.

I have based my life purpose on what brings me joy in life. Because of this, just reading it fires me up and fuels me each and every day.

Your life purpose should trigger a strong obsession within you. It should trigger creative thoughts, drive you to establish huge, ambitious goals, and make you excited to be alive.

Having this sort of passion and obsession will almost certainly culminate in outstanding results and success, regardless of what you decide to do.

"Passion is one of the greatest forces that unleashes creativity, because if you're passionate about something, then you're more willing to take risks."

~ Yo-yo Ma ~

Without this sort of purpose, it is easy to wander aimlessly, zone out, and watch 10 unmemorable years fly by in the blink of an eye.

What does this have to do with leaving the grind behind?

The only way you'll charge at a project with enough enthusiasm to make it through the hurdles, failures, and naysayers is if you are passionate about it. You need to want to succeed with an unlimited amount of desire. Your activity has to be something you *want* to grind for.

Building a foundation of personal purpose gives you the ultimate reason to succeed. Doing what you feel you were put here to do will give you the fuel to do everything it takes to achieve that purpose and leave the grind behind. And by the way, if you're doing things on purpose, you'll enjoy the journey in a completely different way.

So get going on this chapter's actions and habits to get your own life purpose statement in place.

Grinder Summary

1. You are responsible for your life. You are responsible for determining your purpose and legacy.
2. Successful businesses define their purpose; you should too.
3. Think of yourself as the CEO of your life.

4. Having a life purpose keeps you from wasting time on the wrong activities.

5. Want to learn more about establishing a life purpose? Read

6. The Success Principles by Jack Canfield.

Grinder Action:
Determine Your Life Purpose

Your life purpose will serve as the basis for how you lead your life as a Grinder. Your goals and actions will all be aligned with your life purpose. Therefore, this is a highly-individualized action step.

Life purposes can and should change over time. You should therefore consider revisiting this chapter as you hit certain milestones in your life.

This action is a discovery exercise for identifying your purpose. This is the lengthiest exercise in this book, but isn't determining your life purpose a big deal?

Here's how to get your creativity rolling:

1. Make a list of activities that make you happy.

The more you live your life working toward larger meaning and purpose, the happier you will be. Accordingly, what makes you happy is a clue to what your particular purpose in life is.

Write out a list of 10 to 50 items that make you truly happy and blissful.

2. Make a list of the activities that make you excited to get out of bed.

Think back through your life. Write down 10 to 50 times in your life when you stayed up late passionately involved with something, only to wake up bright-eyed and excited to start again. You'll see overlap with the prior list, getting you closer to your life's purpose.

3. Ask why you're unique

If your life purpose is chosen by you and should be different than everyone else's, you had better play to your strengths. What are you very good at relative to other people?

Write down 5 to 10 items.

> **"Strength lies in differences, not in similarities."**
>
> **~ Stephen R. Covey ~**

4. Define your perfect existence.

Assuming you had no limitations, what would your perfect life look like? Write your brief dream story. If everything was perfect, what would your life look like in 10 years? Who is in your life? Where are you living? How do you contribute to society? What do you own? What do you give?

For this exercise, a 1 to 3-page story is ideal.

5. Plug into the rest of the world.

Your life purpose needs to include meaningful interaction and contribution. Who do you want to help? What about your relationships, including your family and friends?

How do you want to help them? Teaching? Donating your time to them? Donating money? How can your unique strengths benefit others?

Weave your answers into your dream story.

6. Narrow the lists.

If you've followed these steps, you've built an impressive list of clues that will help you find your life purpose.

Review what you've written and sleep on it. Give it a night or two for reflection.

7. Write your life purpose.

Now that you've allowed your mind to sift through the great information you have pulled together, it's time to extract your life purpose in the following format:

- I use my unique (include your top unique skills and traits) in order to...
- Create a (list the best parts of your perfect world vision, and ensure you include your impact on others)...
- By (list the activities that make you happy and excited).

This statement will focus your energy and drive on creatively using your talents and doing what you love in order to help yourself and others. That is exciting! If you want to bounce your ideas off of me and get help refining your life purpose statement, send me an email at justin@grindbehindbook.com.

Grinder Habit: Morning Review of Your Life Purpose

A good pilot or astronaut doesn't just jump into their vehicle and go. They review a very important and critical checklist every time. A simple and powerful way to start your day on target is to review your life purpose statement.

Read your life purpose upon waking. This will help remind you of where you want to go, and will therefore make your decisions throughout the day easy and purposeful.

Write it on a notecard for easy access.

CHAPTER 4

Determine Your Grinder 3 Goals

> "Don't set your goals too low. If you don't need much, you won't become much."
>
> ~ Jim Rohn ~

Alright, everyone knows they need goals. You need to set something for yourself to achieve. But do you currently have life-changing goals set for yourself? Crystal clear goals that are written down and can confirm whether or not you succeed?

Many of us pay goals lip service but never really set and focus on goals that will make an impact. One reason for this is people are afraid of failure. If you set a big goal that allows you to determine whether you succeed or not, you will—naturally—know if you are a success or not.

But don't worry about that. You will fail at big goals more often than not. This is exactly why people don't set goals and in particular, don't set big goals—they don't want to risk being a failure.

But by protecting ourselves from failures, we're missing out on something much bigger. I fail and miss my goals all the time. But, even if I miss a goal, I find that I've ended up somewhere much better than where I was before I started or even expected.

Here's something else to consider: people who "hit it big" generally have years of failure behind them. We just don't see that part of their lives. We just see their success and assume, falsely, that they hit everything out of the park. In reality, they are the people who are setting big goals and persisting, failure after failure.

One of the quotes that best illustrates this comes from Michael Jordan:

"I've missed more than 9000 shots in my career. I've lost almost 300 games. 26 times, I've been trusted to take the game winning shot and missed. I've failed over and over and over again in my life. And that is why I succeed."

~ Michael Jordan ~

How to Set MASSIVE Goals

Goals are a key ingredient for living. If you're not regularly setting the right types of goals and working to achieve them, you're plodding through life. And likely you're helping someone else achieve their goals.

Many people don't set any goals at all (Cogs). Many people set goals that are entirely unimpressive (Cogs). And many people don't do what it really takes to achieve their goals (yep, still Cogs).

Don't follow the herd. Set massive goals and actually achieve them. Set goals that will make you a Grinder.

> **"Progress in your life is directly proportional to goals you set. If you are constantly challenging yourself, the growth is there for the taking."**
>
> **~ Salil Gupta ~**

What you'll find here is the consolidation of what I've applied in my own life to achieve big results. This is an amalgam of what I've learned from numerous top-level coaching programs, including Stephen Covey, Jack Canfield, Gary Ryan Blair, Brian Buffini, T Harv Eker, and professional systems such as The Core. These are all highly valuable, yet expensive programs. Here you'll get much of their wisdom distilled into a set of best practices.

Setting Massive Goals is Easy but You're Probably Doing it Wrong

There is a systematic way to set and achieve big goals. This will drastically reduce the time it takes you to achieve goals and increase the results you realize. Nothing is more fulfilling than realizing a life lived on purpose, which is done by setting and achieving massive goals.

How has your goal setting worked out? Have you set S.M.A.R.T. (Specific, Measurable, Achievable, Realistic, and Time-bound) goals? Do you and your boss set annual performance goals? Are you achieving those goals? Were you initially motivated to accomplish those goals? Are you still?

My bet is that most people reading this book are above-average achievers. But most are not really sticking to their goals and accomplishing them. Most people aren't yet making tremendous, game-changing moves.

When you're done with this chapter, you're going to be on your way to setting exciting goals—goals you'll be jazzed about. And you'll learn how to stay motivated to actually see your goal through.

5 Steps to Setting Grinder-Worthy Goals

Setting massive, achievable goals is not complicated, but you may be missing some of the key ingredients that take you from writing something down and shoving it in your desk to actually accomplishing it.

Goal Setting Step 1: Think big. Then think sooner and bigger.

If your goals aren't big enough, they won't require you to make the changes necessary to get different results in your life. It's easy to stagnate in life and get caught up in the daily grind.

It's easy to do the same things day-to-day...work at a monotonous job, watch TV to unwind, go to bed, wake up, and start all over. Years go by in the blink of an eye. Don't waste your life away by setting small goals.

In fact, small goals have a dangerous side-effect. What if you set a goal of earning 10% more next year? Is that achievable without any drastic changes? Probably. What if you set a goal of earning 100% more next year?

Your goals should make you uncomfortable or even nervous. They should get you out of your comfort zone. If you're in your comfort zone, you're not improving. And you're not going to achieve greatness. You should learn to recognize these feelings as a sign you are on the right path.

In fact, a benchmark I use is to consider whether or not I know *how* to achieve a goal I am setting. If I know how to achieve it, the goal isn't big enough.

For example, I know how to purchase another rental home. But do I know how to purchase 10 more rentals homes in the same period? No. In order to do this, I need to get out of my comfort zone.

Some people will argue that big goals are a problem. If your goal is too big, you won't see results and will get discouraged. Or the goal will become so abstract that you will fail to even start. I argue that these are both symptoms of other problems. These are Cog problems.

Grinders figure out what they really want from life and set their goals to achieve it. Period.

Grinders don't let anyone else say their goal is too big or crazy—this is your one life, you are in charge of getting what you want from it.

Big goals are oftentimes no harder to achieve than moderate goals. This is something I never really believed until I experienced it myself.

The best example is a big income goal I set. I also had a goal of maintaining better work-life balance. The problem is I had a belief that high-income levels required sacrificing personal life. But I decided to have goals for both high income and strong work-life balance. I didn't know how it could be done. But the results have been outstanding.

Indeed, the only way I found to achieve this goal was to leave the grind behind. And as you know, I very quickly began earning much more money. I'm working less, having more fun, and achieving the goal of spending more and higher-quality time with my family and friends. A big move was required, but—goal achieved.

I guarantee there are many people who are working much harder than me yet not getting what they want from life simply because the magnitude of their goals is too small. Don't waste your time on small goals. You owe it to yourself to get everything you want out of life.

Speaking of fast, once you've set your big goal, put a time limit on achieving it. Make it soon. You probably already know the amazing power of compound interest on your money--the same principle applies to your personal effort. Every day and year you sit idle, you will achieve massive amounts *less* in your life than you could if you put effort in every day. So get it at. Shift your target dates closer. Achieve daily.

Goal Setting Step 2: Find several authors who have achieved your goal.

Let's continue using money as an example. If you have your eyes set on earning an exceptional amount of money, your next step is to go out and find people who make a lot of money.

Start by looking for people who have written books about your goal. Find inspiration by reading their work and redefining your "what's possible." How did they set their goals? What goals do they consider normal?

This is a very important step for a few reasons:

1. It helps you realize other people have already accomplished your goal.
2. It helps you learn more about how they set and accomplished their goals. It might be drastically different than you expect.

Goal Setting Step 3: Find a personal contact who has achieved your goal already.

Now that you've found authors who have achieved your goal, find someone local who has done the same. Find a real person you can talk to and possibly be mentored by. Call and tell them you want to make a big change in your life and you'd love to take them out to lunch. They will almost certainly say yes.

If this one gets you out of your comfort zone, you'll find much more in Section 2 of this book.

You may think this step is a stretch, but I can tell you nothing will make a bigger difference in getting from where you are now to where you want to be than the people in your network. We all become the average of whom we spend our time with.

Do you want to travel the world? If you found someone who has done so for years, don't you think they'd be helpful? Wouldn't they like to talk about it with someone who is interested? They will shortcut your goal setting and achievement process.

What if you want to be a highly successful real estate investor? What if you could learn from someone local who is an active and successful investor?

These people offer guidance, open doors, and build your network. They will help you set better goals. These are critical steps for taking massive leaps.

Goal Setting Step 4: Find the emotional reasons to achieve your goal.

Something nearly all goal-setting systems miss is the emotional aspect. If you don't have clear emotions tied to your goals, you're missing a key motivator. Emotions provide fuel. They give us a reason.

You can start to identify the emotional reasons to achieve your goals by asking yourself why.

List some great, emotionally-based reasons you want to achieve your goal. Tie your goals to your life-purpose statement.

For example, for my goal of maintaining a certain level of health well into my old age, here are some emotional-based reasons I wrote down:

- My retirement years will be full of adventure. Travel. Community service. Writing. My health will not hold me back! I will not retire and be sedentary. I will not sit in a recliner watching TV all day.
- I will be able to keep up with my son, regardless of his activity level or age.
- My wife and I will have no physical limits on what we do once we have an empty nest. Traveling, living on the beach, whatever we want—our age will not be a limiting factor.

As you can see, I have some long-term motivation to stay fit and healthy. I know there is a cumulative effect. If I am about to skip exercise or eat poorly, I can pause, think of the emotional reasons I set in order to achieve my health goals, and then reconsider my day-to-day decisions.

Goal Setting Step 5: Write out your massive goals.

At this point, you should have a precise idea of what you want your massive goals to be. You should have tools to believe they will be possible.

So let's put some pen to paper. Start writing with the following in mind:

1. Make each goal big and ambitious. The goal should push you out of your comfort zone.
2. When you write the goal, do so in the present tense, as if it is already achieved.
3. The wording should be positive rather than negative. It should have a deadline.
4. Identify a date by which you'd like to complete it. Be aggressive.
5. It should be measurable, which means you should know if it is accomplished. In most cases, include the term "or better" at the end to say you want to achieve a certain goal "or better."
6. Write how you will feel once the goal is accomplished. Now add some glitz, with over-the-top verbiage to spice it up and make your emotional reaction to them more memorable. What are those emotions you're tapping into?
7. Include what you will do in exchange, such as work hard, reach thousands of people, or give your full dedication.

If I put this all together in terms of a monetary goal, it would look something like:

"I have a net worth of $1.8 million or more by December 31st. I feel excited, fulfilled, and beyond proud as a result--my family is happy and secure, and we're poised to live the life we want without compromise. In exchange, I worked harder, smarter, and faster than everyone else. I took massive action daily. I executed game-changing business ideas."

How do you tailor goals toward leaving the grind behind?

As I began focusing more deliberately on writing out my goals, I quickly realized that achieving them all together in my current circumstances was *impossible*. I wanted to make much more money. I wanted passive cash flow. I wanted more time for my family. I wanted to follow my passions. I wanted to achieve *my* goals, not someone else's.

Why is this incompatible with holding a standard job? It should be fairly obvious, but I'll explain. I was making an excellent income, but was it reasonable to double my income? Mapping out salary increases, promotions, and gaining a better understanding of what those above me earned made me greatly question what my true earning potential was in Corporate America.

Further, if I did move into a higher position, I would effectively be married to my company. My superiors slogged through a life of travel, long hours, and a "company first" mentality. This reality was not in my goal set or aligned with my life purpose. It didn't lead to a balanced life. It didn't jive with my values.

As I analyzed how I could achieve my goals, it became very obvious I needed to change my situation. I needed to transition from a Cog to a Grinder.

Could you also set a goal to explicitly leave the grind behind? Absolutely. For me, it was a natural extension of my other goals and became its own goal very quickly.

Grinder Summary

1. If you're not setting goals, how do you know where you're going and what you'll need to change in your life?
2. Goals need to be massive. Cogs set uninspiring goals.
3. Grinders set massive goals that require situation upheaval.
4. Finding someone who has already achieved your goal is a big—often ignored—step.
5. Emotion is power. All goals need emotional juice.
6. Want to learn more about setting and achieving goals? Read *The Compound Effect* by Darren Hardy.

Grinder Action: Create Your GRINDER 3 Goals

This action is a pivotal moment in this book. In this section, you will set goals and then pick your top 3, which we'll coin your GRINDER 3. These are your critical goals: goals that you will grind through every day until they are accomplished.

This chapter was full of exercise-oriented information; now it is time to put that information into practice. It's time to write down your goals using the steps I describe below.

As you write your goals, remember these key ingredients:

1. Make each goal big and ambitious. The goal should push you out of your comfort zone.
2. When you write the goal, do so in the present tense as if it is already achieved.
3. The wording should be positive rather than negative.
4. It should have a deadline. Identify a date you'd like to complete it by. Be aggressive.
5. It should be measurable, which means you should know if it is accomplished. In most cases, include the term "or better" at the end to say you want to achieve a certain goal "or better."
6. Write how you will feel once the goal is accomplished. Now add some glitz, with over-the-top verbiage to spice it up and make your emotional reaction to them more memorable. What are those emotions you're tapping into?
7. Include what you will do in exchange, such as work hard, reach thousands of people, or give your full dedication.
8. And remember, think big. Then think bigger and sooner.

You should now pick your top 3 goals. These are the goals that will make the biggest difference in your life. These are your GRINDER 3. These goals will be the key things you will focus on. Write them down on notecards.

Once you have your GRINDER 3, I recommend challenging yourself to write a total of 100 goals. This is difficult but great fun! It forces you to really dig into what you want from life, and I encourage you to stretch for the full 100 goals.

These goals don't require the focus your GRINDER 3 will, but it's great to have them stored in a notebook somewhere. As you come back over time, you might be shocked at how many you knock out.

Grinder Habit:
Morning Review of Your GRINDER 3

Now that you have your goals written down, it's time to put them to work. Goals are most effective when they are burned into your brain and positively consume you. You should be obsessed with your goals.

> "I'd rather be really hokey and really rich than really cool and really broke."
>
> ~ T. Harv Eker ~

You are already starting your morning off on purpose. By adding a daily review of your goals, you are further guiding yourself and your actions for the day.

Take out the notecards containing your GRINDER 3 and read them to yourself...every morning...without fail. If you are more adventurous and don't mind seeming a tad silly, the best way to do this is to read your cards out loud in front of a mirror. While this might seem hokey, it will engage additional senses, making for a more complete and memorable experience.

CHAPTER 5

Advertise Success To Yourself

Stop! Did you set your GRINDER 3 goals? If not, go back and complete the Grinder Action in chapter 5. Your GRINDER 3 are a pre-requisite for the remainder of this book

Alright, let's start this chapter off right with a fantastic quote that drives home the seriousness of its concept:

> "FACT: Your brain is being controlled-and you don't even know it."
>
> ~Drew Eric Whitman,The Nation's #1 Advertising-Effectiveness Trainer ~

Let's get you in control. It's time to take back control of your brain. It's time to leverage the power of advertising on yourself. *Sell yourself on success.*

Using Advertisements for Success

The term "affirmations" has become a dirty word in the world of "real success." Affirmations have been associated with wishful thinking and pseudo-science. In fact, affirmations have such a stigma, I decided I needed to use the term "Advertisement" in the name of this chapter.

It's a shame there is a stigma.

Affirmations are in fact highly powerful, and when used right, are a key ingredient in your overall success picture.

Consider this chapter the ultimate guide to using affirmations to achieve success. I'll discuss the reality of affirmations and how you can play the mental game toward your advantage. They are a key tool that helps you change results in most aspects of your life. They are exceptionally effective at helping you make a massive change…a change such as leaving the grind behind.

> "If I've learned anything in life, it is that if you believe something is possible, you tend to focus on the constructive means necessary to make that possibility a reality. I've also learned to believe the opposite. If you don't think something is possible, then you will be blinded to the ways it could be done. It's like a self- imposed blind spot."
>
> ~ Gary Keller, co-founder of Keller Williams Realty International - The Millionaire Real Estate Agent ~

Want some proof that affirmations work? Look no further than the $100B US advertising industry. Has your behavior ever been swayed by an advertisement? No doubt. The core tool of advertising is repetitive messaging that drives your behavior in the advertiser's favor. That, my friend, is affirmative power at work.

Why not use the same methodology to shape your mind the way you want it to be shaped? You can use affirmations to drive your subconscious behavior toward achieving what you want.

> "Did you know that teams of skilled consumer psychologists routinely consult with ad agencies to help them construct ads that powerfully affect consumers on a psychological, even subconscious level? It's true! Don't be alarmed...that's what advertising is all about!"
>
> ~ Drew Eric Whitman, Cashvertising ~

Do my mind's subconscious beliefs drive my behavior and results?

Absolutely. All of us have a mindset or preconception about how the world works, what we are worth, and how we fit in. This preconception drives much of our behavior. Therefore, changing your preconception will change both your behavior and your results. After all, your current life situation is the sum result of your previous actions, decisions, and beliefs.

> "Sooner or later, those who win are those
> who think they can."
>
> ~ Richard Bach ~

Affirmations are a key tool that helps you focus on your goals and make achieving them more believable. Affirmations allow you to change your beliefs. They are simple messages you repeat to yourself, and over time, they recondition your fundamental, subconscious thoughts about yourself and your capabilities.

If you're setting goals that seem unbelievable, doesn't it seem that affirmations will help you transition to finding them believable?

> "Confront old conditioning. It leads to unconscious behavior....Examine your core beliefs. Hold them up to the light and discard beliefs that make you stuck. ... Your brain must become your ally. If it does not, it will remain your adversary"
>
> ~ Depak Chopka, MD, and Rudolph Tanzi, PhD, Super Brain ~

Advertisers use affirmations on you

Everyone knows the company McDonalds, yet McDonalds continues to advertise constantly and aggressively. Why? This repetitive messaging will, given enough time, change your behavior and trigger you to make purchases at McDonalds. Again and again. This is the power of affirmations, and you need to begin using that power on yourself to create your own story!

How has your mind been shaped over time?

You have been receiving messages about how things should be your entire life. Growing up, these messages came from your parents, teachers, your community, and other influential people in your life.

As you mature, your friends, environment, coworkers, and the media heavily influence your beliefs. Who or what is shaping your mind now, without you even knowing it? Are you watching hours of commercials every day and letting others build your sense of self?

Are you a marketing-victim Cog, or are you ready to take the driver's seat and become a self-directed Grinder?

Have you ever noticed confident people are successful and get what they want? This is because they naturally define their own self-image and don't allow the beliefs and expectations of others to determine their limits and beliefs. Confident people self-affirm their own beliefs and therefore achieve greatness.

The good news is you can use affirmations to alter the beliefs that don't support your life purpose and goals.

What Exactly are Self-Advertisements?

Self-advertisements are simple, memorable, statements that you read and/or listen to multiple times per day. They are affirmations.

The goal is to begin believing whatever it is the affirmations tell you. They are mental commercials that sell your best self to your current self.

To put affirmations to work, you write short sentences that challenge the way you currently perceive the world. As you repeatedly read these sentences, you begin to alter your perceptions. This change in perception then translates into a change in your real-world results.

For example, if you believe your $20,000 per year salary is normal and that a $100,000 per year salary is unachievable, you need an affirmation. The affirmation will be one component of your metamorphosis from a $20k earner to a six-figure earner.

Or what if you think people who earn very large amounts of money are bad? Or that your weight problem is due to family genetics? These types of beliefs will not help you change. They'll keep you where you are today.

Affirmations allow you to replace doubtful, negative, or uncertain, "*this* is normal," and "can't do" thoughts and replace them with positive, affirmative, "*that* can be my normal," and "can do" thoughts.

> "Change your self-talk and your comfort zone by affirmations. Bombard your subconscious mind with new thoughts and images. In each area of life, create at least one affirmation."
>
> ~ Jack Canfield, The Success Principles ~

What can affirmations help me accomplish?

Since life is a mental game, using affirmations has broad implications. A Grinder should use written affirmations for each major part of life, including:

Health Affirmations

Include such items as weight, strength, cardiovascular fitness, and more. *I am healthy, toned, stress free, and youthful.*

Wealth Affirmations

Include earnings, net worth, streams of income, effort to earn, and more. Money comes to me often and easily, giving me the freedom to live life however I want.

Relationship Affirmations

Include how you want to spend time with your family, friends, and coworkers. What does your ideal relationship look like? *I enjoy spending every day with my incredibly beautiful spouse and children. Together, we live a joyful life.*

Career and Creative Affirmations

Include what you want to achieve in your career, how hard you have to work for it, and what you need to get there. I am action oriented, turning ideas into measurable results quickly and often. I realize this outstanding success while enjoying a balanced life.

Community Affirmations

Include how you can benefit your community, how you can increase and enhance your contributions, relationships, and more. I only think positive thoughts about those around me and assume others have the best intentions. I give my time to the benefit of another at least once per day.

What does research say?

There is a lot of great research on affirmations, but I urge you to read Yale's publication *The Unconscious Mind* by John A. Bargh and Ezequiel Morsella.

"This research has demonstrated the existence of several independent unconscious behavioral guidance systems: perceptual, evaluative, and motivational. From this perspective, it is concluded that in both phylogeny and ontogeny, actions of an unconscious mind precede the arrival of a conscious mind—that action precedes reflection."

~ Yale research ~

As published in Psychological Science, a journal of the Association of Psychological Science, the actual effects of affirmations are real and measurable.

"Although we know that self-affirmation reduces threat and improves performance, we know very little about why this happens. And we know almost nothing about the neural correlates of this effect," says lead researcher

~ Lisa Legault of Clarkson University. ~

Do successful and famous people use affirmations?

While it's certainly a stretch to say all successful people use affirmations, there are plenty who credit affirmative beliefs as key components of their success, particularly as they transitioned from rough times to lucrative ones.

Jim Carrey utilized affirmations to help him break into acting.

> "I am a really good actor. I have all kinds of great movie offers. Movie offers are out there for me, I just don't hear them yet."

Oprah Winfrey regularly discusses her use of affirmations.

> "If you believe you can only go so far, it is an obstacle."

Arnold Schwarzenegger used affirmations heavily to help realize successful bodybuilding, film, and political careers.

> "The more I focused in on this image and worked and grew, the more I saw it was real and possible for me to be like him."

"It's the same process I used in bodybuilding,... What you do is create a vision of who you want to be, and then live into that picture as if it were already true."

"I'm going to be the number-one box-office star in all of Hollywood."

Henry Ford was famous for surrounding himself with people who used mental tricks.

"I am looking for a lot of men who have an infinite capacity to not know what can't be done."

"If you think you can do a thing or think you can't do a thing, you're right."

Alex Noble recognizes success is a process that includes affirmations.

"Success is a process, a quality of mind and way of being, an outgoing affirmation of life."

Napoleon Hill spent two decades studying the 500 most successful people in the world, and determined the mental game, including affirmations, was the key to success.

> "Any idea, plan, or purpose may be placed in the mind through repetition of thought."

> "Here is a most significant fact—the subconscious mind takes any orders given it in a spirit of absolute FAITH, and acts upon those orders, although the orders often have to be presented over and over again, through repetition, before they are interpreted by the subconscious mind."

W. Clement Stone taught many—including Jack Canfield—about affirmations.

> "Self-suggestion makes you master of yourself."

Dr Maxwell Maltz details how affirmations integrate with behavior.

> "This same creative mechanism within you can help you achieve your best possible 'self' if you will form a picture in your imagination of the self you want to be and 'see yourself' in the new role."

Will Smith regularly discusses his use of affirmations, which include this great quote:

> "The first step is you have to say that you can. Believing in yourself is the first step to accomplishing any goal. If you think you're going to fail, you probably will."

Targeted affirmations

What if you have a goal to reduce your body fat to 10%, but your family is all overweight? If you believe being overweight is in your genes, that limiting belief (albeit inaccurate) is an obstacle that will prevent you from achieving your goal.

Similarly, what if you want to make $300,000 per year, but you don't have a college degree? If you believe you need a degree to achieve that sort of salary, you've created a limiting, inaccurate belief that will hinder you from achieving your goal.

Therefore, your job is to identify what beliefs are keeping you from accomplishing what you want in life. You then create affirmations that directly tackle those beliefs. Since your mind is at the root of everything you do, affirmations can help you change results in any aspect of your life.

The 3 top books on affirmations

Affirmations are a fascinating topic. The full story of them is outside the scope of this book, so I'd like to recommend a few books that really dive deep into the science behind them. Since I said there is a lot of junk and pseudo-science "baggage" associated with affirmations, I want to be particular about the list to read.

As a skeptic myself, it was important for me to get over this baggage and understand affirmations in a deeper manner.

1. *Psycho Cybernetics* by Dr Maxwell Maltz. Written by a doctor and based on his field research, this book provides a fantastic overview of affirmations and the mental game. There is no better resource.

2. *Super Brain* by Rudolph E. Tanzi Ph.D. and Deepak Chopra. This book provides a Harvard Medical School Professor's outstanding perspective of the power of the mind.

3. *The Success Principles* by Jack Canfield. This book places affirmations in a broader self-improvement context.

Grinder Summary

1. Affirmations have been oversold, made hokey, and become stigmatized. What a shame.

2. Want some proof that affirmations work? Look no further than the $100B US advertising industry.

3. Research shows the actual effects of affirmations are real and measurable.

4. Affirmations are a key tool that help you focus on your goals and make achieving them more believable.

5. Are you a marketing-victim Cog, or are you ready to get into the driver's seat and become a self-directed Grinder?

6. Want to know more about affirmations? Read *Super Brain* by Depak Chopka, MD, and Rudolph Tanzi, PhD

Grinder Action: Write your Own Grinder Affirmations

It's time to put pen to paper again. This exercise will walk you through creating your first set of highly effective affirmations.

Don't worry about gearing these affirmations toward "leaving the grind behind;" rather, think through the questions in each of these steps.

1. Think about your goals in life

For each GRINDER 3, write down the beliefs that keep you from taking action today. Secondly, write down the beliefs keep you from making your goal much, much bigger. Focus on these beliefs. We want to change those beliefs! Some examples:

- I cannot make a lot of money without working excessively.
- I can't quit my job! I have a mortgage, car payments, mouths to feed, etc…
- I can't have both a successful marriage and a highly successful career.

- In order to leave the grind behind, I'm going to have to sell, and I'm not good at persuading people.

If you don't feel you have a belief holding you back from achieving a goal in a particular area of life, ask yourself if you are truly taking sufficient action to achieve that goal. If you're not taking action on the goal, dig deeper and create an affirmation to get the ball rolling.

2. Identify negative self-images

In this step, identify negative self-images or negative thoughts you have about yourself. What skills, traits, genes, or other personal factor do you believe you are lacking? Some examples:

- I am overweight.
- Nobody at work respects my opinion.
- I didn't graduate from college, so I can't earn six figures.
- Most people work boring Cog jobs and seem happy enough.
- Settling seems like an okay way to live.

3. Define how you want the world to work

Now, turn these beliefs on their heads and define how you want the world to work. Some examples:

- I can make a lot of money without working excessively.
- I can have a happy, successful marriage and a highly successful career.
- I am beautiful and at a perfect, healthy weight.

- People at work highly respect my opinions.

4. Start your affirmations with "I am…"

Affirmations are about altering your beliefs; you are in charge of yourself. Do not try to change someone else. Take ownership and start your affirmations with "I."

5. You are in charge—no limits!

Do not limit yourself. The world is open. You dictate how the world works. Do not think your affirmations are ridiculous. Similar to goals, also keep your affirmations open-ended by adding words like "or better." *I am readily capable of making $500,000 or better this year.*

6. Ramp up. Affirmations should be big yet believable.

Affirmations should push you out of your comfort zone yet should be believable. To attain to a very large goal, you can progressively grow your affirmations as you take steps toward your goal. Gaining momentum is critical to a success plan.

7. Positive wording = positive results from affirmations

The wording should be positive rather than negative. Positive thoughts and attitudes lead to success and opportunity. Rather than

"I *don't* have fat genes," say "I *am* fully in control of becoming superbly lean."

8. Add words of emotion and feeling to your affirmations

As with goals, when you add emotional triggers, your affirmations will be more memorable, more fun to read, and will work with your mind on a deeper level. Think about effective advertisements. They are catchy, easy to remember, and play on our emotions.

9. Use your own research to enhance your belief

Chances are someone else has come from your circumstance and achieved the result you want. Do you want to be a millionaire but have recently declared bankruptcy? Here you see further overlap with your GRINDER 3 goals. If you haven't already, read about people who have already been there and done that. This will *prove* to you it is possible. Now you just need to tell yourself it is possible for you too.

10. Consolidate everything into a sentence or two

Now that you have your thoughts together, hand write your affirmation in a single sentence or two. Something you can easily read to yourself with regularity.

Examples of Affirmations

I am running an extremely successful business that brings me huge sums of money, while also providing high degrees of personal satisfaction and freedom.

In my career, I will have flexible hours and be able to spend awesomely high- quality time with friends and family.

I am doing so well, I can give $250,000 or more to charity.

I am confident and positive that everything will unfold perfectly in my life.

My future is unfolding perfectly. My life will be filled with abundance, success, and joy.

I am toned, lean, and feeling fantastic! I am strong, healthy, and always young.

I am an absolute money magnet, netting $380,000 or more per year through my own business ventures.

Money comes to me often and easily.

I am beyond proud to have built a net worth of $2,300,000.

I am a positive thinker. My mind

is filled every day with positive thoughts, creating a beautiful and positive life for me.

Write out your affirmations

You have all of the information you need to get going! Grab a piece of paper. Think about where you want to be in life. Write 20 total affirmations.

Of these 20 affirmations, pick the top 3 that will most impact your GRINDER 3 goals.

Grinder Habit: Affirmations Routine

Now that you have your affirmations, it's time to put them into practice.

The habits to this point are slotted for specific times of the day. With affirmations, though, I prefer to review them throughout the day in different ways—just as though they were playing on the radio or TV.

1. Review your notecard-based affirmations spontaneously throughout the day.

2. Record your affirmations and listen to them as you drive.

3. Visualize your affirmations by cutting out pictures of supporting imagery.

CHAPTER 6

Visualize Success

Both this chapter and the next deal with two highly related concepts: visualization and the subconscious. The subconscious is a remarkably powerful tool that is seldom utilized. Here, you will see how to employ it and direct it. But to do so, you first need extreme clarity into what you are trying to achieve, which is best accomplished with visualization—opening the mind's eye.

In fact, the trick to doing this is shockingly simple. You visualize that you've already completed your goal. By doing this, you activate the power of your subconscious. But, there are many subtleties to doing this properly. So here we go.

It's time to get visualization working in your favor, employing your subconscious to turn you into an efficient, effective Grinder.

What is Visualization?

Visualization is a form of meditation in which you see yourself achieving a particular goal. This can be as simple as seeing yourself take a successful golf swing or as complicated as seeing yourself earning $500,000.

Like affirmations, visualization works to condition your mind toward a desired outcome. But it also does something else—it imparts within your mind a high degree of clarity. It requires you to see exactly what you want. If you're not sure where you're going, do you think you'll get there? No.

Visualization cements your destination. It provides the GPS coordinates for your mind. Once your mind knows where it's going, its awesome potential is unleashed.

Goal achievement with visualization is heavily utilized in sports

It is fairly common knowledge that visualization is a highly effective technique for improving physical and athletic outcomes. Many successful athletes have coaches specifically for visualization, whether they participate in Olympic events, basketball, golf, boxing, or otherwise.

> "I never hit a shot, not even in practice, without having a very sharp, in-focus picture of it in my head. First I see the ball where I want it to finish, nice and white and sitting up high on the bright green grass. Then the scene quickly changes, and I see the ball going there; its path, trajectory, and shape, even its behavior on landing."
>
> ~ Jack Nicklaus ~

The University of Chicago performed the quintessential visualization study in which basketball free throw improvement was measured. Participants were divided into three groups. After establishing baseline free-throw accuracy, each group implemented a different improvement plan for the next 30 days.

Group 1 physically shot free throws to improve their skill. Group 2 used visualization to mentally shoot free throws to improve their skill. Group 3 did nothing to improve. The results were astonishing:

- Group 1 used traditional physical practice, and improved accuracy by 24%
- Group 2 used mental visualization practice *only*, and improved accuracy by 23%
- Group 3 did not practice, and showed no improvement.

This study proves that you can teach your body to perform physical feats better just by properly visualizing improved outcomes. In fact, the improvement achieved by practicing in the mind was no statistically different than practicing physically. The transference from mental to physical was essentially 100%.

Does visualization work outside of sports?

"The key to effective visualization is to create the most detailed, clear and vivid a picture to focus on as possible. The more vivid the visualization, the more likely, and quickly, you are to begin attracting the things that help you achieve what you want to get done."

~ Georges St Pierre in The Way of the Fight ~

Georges St Pierre is one of my favorite athletes. Apart from achieving incredible success in his sport, he is also a tremendously successful person outside of the sport. He has built a financial kingdom, become an incredible role model, and is a key ambassador for change.

Georges St Pierre uses visualization for both physical and non-physical outcomes. He credits visualization as a key part of his overall life success.

This concept applies directly to your GRINDER 3 goals. Realizing a major goal, passing an exam, or giving a killer presentation are fairly different than shooting a free throw. Visualization in sports is largely about getting your conscious mind to spend less time over-dictating to your muscles and instead allowing your body to figure out the best way to coordinate and achieve your goal.

For example, when you take a step forward, do you specifically ask each muscle to contract by a certain amount, consciously driving every little action through the process? Or do you just think about the bigger picture—where you want to go? People very commonly over-think minute muscle actions in sports when, instead, they should mentally provide their body a goal to achieve.

Much like you ask your body to move forward, you should ask your body to sink that putt. Micro-managing of movement is the problem but can be corrected by using visualization to focus on the big-picture physical task rather than the thousands of small tasks it takes to move properly.

Visualization for non-physical goals works in the exact same way. It is about seeing the end-state and big picture rather than the thousands of tasks and obstacles that stand in your way.

It is about how to achieve the big without tripping over the small. How many times have you wanted to do something big yet never even started because you were overwhelmed by small issues? Visualization is a key ingredient in overcoming this problem.

So what's the key to using successful visualization to improve mental outcomes?

Introduction to iterative visualization

While visualization is a powerful tool for goal achievement, it can be challenging. Many of us cannot just close our eyes and really see a detailed scenario. This is why I recommend taking a stair-step, iterative approach. Over time, you build a clearer and deeper picture in your mind of the achievement of a desired goal.

Iterative visualization is a mental-imagery technique used to focus your mind on a desired outcome. It is characterized by short sessions that progressively improve the clarity of the same mental image.

How to Use Visualization for Your GRINDER 3 Goals

Based on what you've read so far, it should be apparent how visualization can aid in achieving your GRINDER 3 goals. You'll also find another benefit, which is that until you try to visualize, you don't know how well you actually understand your goals. Visualization will force you to become clear about what you want.

Visualization, done iteratively, is a fairly easy task and should be done in short time windows. Each time you perform conscious work toward achieving a goal, you should also set aside a few minutes for visualization.

Visualization doesn't need to be done anywhere in particular; in fact, if you limit yourself to having a perfectly quiet room with candles, you're setting yourself up to miss many opportunities for visualization sessions. Instead, perform your visualization wherever you can find a convenient place to sit quietly for a few minutes and close your eyes.

The exercise

To help you get started, you'll want to visualize what happens when you achieve one of your GRINDER 3 goals. Pick one and ponder the question, *"Where will I be when I achieve my goal?"*

Will you be at your computer when you watch your net worth hit a target? Will you be hitting "send" on the announcement to your company that you just quit your Cog job? Perhaps you realize your goal is achieved and run out to hug your spouse with jubilant energy. These are the sorts of situations you can easily use for this exercise.

Here are the steps you should take to get started.

First session (5 minutes):

1. Close your eyes
2. Set the stage. This means thinking about the physical place you will be once your goal is achieved. If you're taking a test, where will you be when you see your results? If you are closing a sale, where will you be when you obtain the signed paperwork? At this stage, aim for a generalized picture of where you will be. You will add detail in later sessions; this is an iterative process.
3. Now, see your own body from your own eyes. Make the
4. visualization first person. After seeing the room or physical location I'm in, I usually like to look down and visualize my hands. If you're having trouble with this, open your eyes and get in the proper posture. If you will be sitting at your computer when your goal is accomplished, go sit down and put your hands on a keyboard. Soak in what this looks like. Then close your eyes and see that same picture.

5. Stop! If you can generally visualize where you'll be when

6. your goal is accomplished and can see part of your body, that's good enough for the first session.

Second session (5 minutes, performed later that same day or the next):

1. Close your eyes and let your mind take you back to where you left off last time. You'll find this gets easier and easier. Soon, you'll be able to snap back to where you left off—with exceptional detail. For now, try your best but don't worry if you don't get this the first time,

2. Once you're settled and relaxed, start looking around your virtual room. Add more details about your surroundings and yourself. Look around and add just a bit at a time.

3. What do you hear and smell?

4. Are there other people in the room?

5. What will you experience to indicate the goal is complete?

6. Imagine turning your head. What else do you see? Scour the scene.

7. Stop! Remember exactly what you saw by taking a mental snapshot. You will be shocked by how well you recall the scene later.

Remaining sessions (5 minutes or so each):

1. You can determine the frequency with which you do these sessions. Perform them at least once per day, but you may prefer more. As you see, these sessions are short.

2. During each session, continue to add detail to your surroundings. My visualizations generally take 5 to 10 sessions before I really start seeing the picture with full, crisp, "HD" type detail. Ultimately, my visualization literally looks like a highly-detailed movie.

3. As your scene evolves, add emotions. Specifically, start adding victorious emotions, layer by layer. What does it feel like when you've accomplished your goal? How does it feel to pass that test? How does it feel to close that sale? As I've said throughout these chapters, emotions are critical. They trigger a deeper mind and memory connection.

4. Extend those emotions to goal-achieved celebrations. See yourself receiving the passing test grade. Bang on the desk in excitement! Run outside! Call your spouse! See the celebration pan out. This should cause you to actually smile as you visualize. This part is critical. And remember, this is all iterative, so the night before you go to the exam or give the presentation, the celebratory visualization celebration should nearly have you jumping out of your chair in excitement because it feels so real.

That is how the sessions unfold. You will continue your visualization, building detail as you go. Take your time and revisit the scene daily, or even many times per day. *You will be amazed how you can take a fuzzy concept and turn it into a crystal-clear mental simulation that feels completely real.*

You have now given your mind a fully defined outcome. Your brain knows *exactly* where you want to go. It will begin doing everything in its power to get you there.

Should I visualize "how" to achieve goals?

Did you notice there is no mention of visualizing the "how?" You are only visualizing the end state, not how to get there. You and your subconscious will work on the *how* separately. Your subconscious will do this by causing you to wake up with inspirational, brilliant ideas filled with things you need to do and people you need to meet. You will be brimming with motivation.

Your job in iterative visualization is to focus on the achieved goal: your end-state.

If you have a hard time with detailed visualization

Some people have trouble closing their eyes and visualizing their surroundings. They have a hard time seeing an environment, and they have an even harder time feeling emotion.

While visualization may not be easy for everyone, it is undoubtedly very valuable. Rather than giving up, I recommend trying exercises to see if you can improve your abilities. Specifically, I recommend reading *The Master Key System* by Charles F. Hannel. It's packed full of exercises specifically designed to improve your visualization capabilities.

Grinder
Summary

1. Use visualization to gain clarity about your GRINDER 3 goals. Until you try to visualize, you don't know how well you actually understand your goals.

2. Visualization is a pre-requisite for leveraging your subconscious, which you'll learn about in the next chapter.

3. Visualization allows you to focus on the big picture and minimize small obstacles. Just like you don't want your conscious mind to over-dictate physical moves in sports, you do not want to get lost in the thousands of details and hurdles between you and your goal of leaving the grind behind.

4. Visualization is a challenging process. Do it in short bursts and expect to add detail over time.

5. Not everyone can use visualization easily. If you want help increasing your capabilities, I recommend checking out *The Master Key System.*

Grinder Action:
Put Visualization to Work

This chapter is filled with action-oriented information, so let's get to it. Identify the GRINDER 3 goal that you feel *least* likely to accomplish. Which goal is out of sight? You'd love to achieve it, but you don't even know where to start. Perhaps you cannot imagine what your life would be like if you accomplished it.

Take that goal and put some deliberate effort into understanding what your life would look like once you've accomplished it. Go through the iterative visualization process identified in this chapter to get the ball rolling. Your goal is to get to the point where you can actually understand and "see" what it would be like to accomplish this goal.

Grinder Habit:
Daily Visualization of GRINDER 3

1. Spend a daily iterative visualization session on your toughest GRINDER 3 goal. See the end state and build up to full clarity.
2. Perform and track visualization sessions, such that you're doing them at least once daily.
3. Keep each session to about 5 minutes.

CHAPTER 7

Leverage Your Subconscious

"He must have a burning desire to solve the problem. But after he has defined the problem, sees in his imagination the desired end result, secured all the information and facts that he can, then additional struggling fretting and worrying over it does not help but seems to hinder the solution."

~ Maxwell Maltz, Psycho-Cybernetics, A New Way to Get More Living Out of Life ~

At this point in the book, you should have realized that the intention of these mental "tricks" is to sharply define—to yourself—what you really want from life. These habits and exercises are all about intense mental focus. This is the sort of focus and obsession required to do something huge like leaving the grind behind.

Over the last chapter, we've been preparing you to marshal a critical ally within your own head: your subconscious. In fact, your subconscious will handle the most complex and difficult problems you face, whether creative or logical. It's just awaiting a clear assignment.

With the tools and habits you've put in place, you're steps away from driving the incredible potential within your brain toward your goal of leaving the grind behind.

Subconscious and delegation

Most people will agree that both delegation and teamwork are key components of life, leadership, and success. A team of people is better than one person. You may excel at tracking your finances yet be in awe of another person's ability to paint.

I probably don't need to argue the benefits of delegating to and engaging with other people to solve problems. However, I'm certain most of us are not effectively reaping the benefits of *internal* delegation.

"It is well understood in psychology that the subconscious mind has the dominant influence on human decision making, and therefore the pivotal role of the subconscious, for you to achieve success, is inescapable."

~ Kevin Michel ~

What if I told you that there is in fact someone available to you right now to work as your partner? Someone to whom you can delegate your biggest challenges and most important tasks. Someone who will transform you into a grinder. And they'll do it for free. There is, in fact, just such an untapped resource right within you.

Introduction to Your Subconscious

How many times have you stared at a computer screen for hours on end, frustrated and stuck? That darn blinking cursor staring back at you. Perhaps you were looking at a complex spreadsheet and couldn't get the numbers to jive. Perhaps you were writing a paper or building a presentation. We've all been there—we hit a mental wall and conscious effort seems to get us nowhere.

Personally, I've spent many hours over the years being actively stuck on problems, even insignificant ones. Giving into frustration, and assuming I was just tired, I'd give up for the day. The problem would be bugging me throughout the evening, and potentially even making it difficult for me to sleep at night.

Then I'd wake up the next day, or maybe later that week, and BAM! The breakthrough answer would invariably come to me while I was brushing my teeth or taking a shower—*while my conscious mind was focused on something else entirely.* Sound familiar?

> "Never go to sleep without a request to your subconscious"
>
> ~ Thomas Edison ~

In fact, many of my best plans "pop" into my head while I'm doing something else entirely. Marketing experiments, product plans, and communications never materialized while I was actively working on them. Rather, once I stop working and switch to another activity—such as sleeping, showering, exercising, or playing—the magic seems to occur.

I talked to others about this phenomenon and thought about it myself but never really knew how to control it. It just seemed to be nothing more than *random inspiration*.

However, as I dug into the research and books on this subject, I learned this phenomenon is a result of a difference between the actively controlled part of my brain and the subconscious part. And most interesting, it was actually something I could *direct* and use to my benefit.

Indeed, this feeling of inspiration *is not random*; it is a mechanism afforded to your body that can be managed and leveraged.

> "Whatever we plant in our subconscious mind and nourish with repetition and emotion will one day become reality."
>
> ~ Earl Nightinglae ~

Your subconscious likes to keep it simple

While others may define the subconscious in alternate ways, for the purposes of this book, think of it as the part of your brain that works on problems while you aren't actively thinking about them.

In these terms, the subconscious is simple. It requires clear, concise direction from your active mind. And then it needs to be left alone.

As Dr. Maxwell Maltz characterizes it, think of your subconscious as a heat-seeking missile. You give your subconscious a target, and then it will blast off and scream toward hitting that target. Rather than manually steering the missile to its goal, you simply supply it a target. It will automatically make constant adjustments and course corrections. It will ultimately find its own best path.

Are you starving your subconscious?

Most of us live cluttered lives, barraged by email, IM, phone calls, and meetings. We then overcompensate by filling the other portion with mindless activities in order to escape the clutter. This sort of scenario confuses your subconscious, and if your best delegate is disconnected and confused, it will have no way to know what target to focus on. Here are some ways you may be short-changing your subconscious.

Do you:

- Go to bed with a long, disorganized to-do list on your mind?

- Go to bed with *no* to-do list in mind?
- Spend a lot of time consuming mindless TV?
- Surf the Internet and social media aimlessly?

Your subconscious can solve most any problem for you, or it can deliver the inspiration you need. But if you're not giving clear direction, it won't do jack. Worse, giving no direction at all will cause your subconscious to fade into the background, leading to boredom, restlessness, and many other problems.

How to Use Your Subconscious

There are four very simple steps to using your subconscious. Before we begin, it's good to apply the delegation analogy one more time.

Think about how you delegate to other intelligent people. You give them a clear picture of the *desired outcome* and then let them go to work. You let them fill in the blanks. You don't micromanage, overwhelm, or constantly change what you want. With that in mind, here are the four steps I use to best leverage my subconscious as a valued delegate.

Step 1: Name and personalize your delegate.

This one may sound cheesy, but makes visualizing the handoff from your conscious mind to your subconscious easy. I named my subconscious "Grinder Jeeves."

Jeeves is a classic servant/butler name—perfect for someone who will be there, devoted to supporting you. But for me, Jeeves brings to mind a stuffy person. I need a little more grit and edge. Naming him "Grinder Jeeves" adds the cool factor. He's Jeeves with sunglasses. That's how to make visualization easy and fun.

Pick a name for your subconscious. Once you have a name, build a complete visual of what this person looks like. Make this personification something you can delegate projects to with the utmost confidence.

You will give your Grinder Jeeves a task and then visualize him walking out the door and not coming back until the job is done with the best of skill. This step is about being able to "see" and relate to your subconscious as a person.

If you prefer a committee work on your problem, even better. Just ensure you're able to visualize this team of Grinder Jeeves that goes to work for you.

> "It is a common experience that a problem difficult at night is resolved in the morning after the committee of sleep has worked on it."
>
> ~ John Steinbeck ~Step 2:

Step 2: Pick 3-5 things you want to accomplish tomorrow.

You are now ready to choose what you want to delegate. There is a very simple way to come up with this list. At the end of your day, sit down and write out the 3 to 5 things that, if accomplished tomorrow, would make you feel completely satisfied with your productivity and output. Pick ones related to your GRINDER 3.

If you knock out 3–5 important things every day, you will accomplish a lot over time thanks to compounding. Consistently achieving this level of output can be challenging, but if you break your long-term goals down into immediate steps, you will be much more successful at them. Whereas a goal of driving across the country may be daunting, driving one mile at a time is not. So for your subconscious to deliver the most value, figure out what those 3–5 things are for tomorrow only.

There are certain key characteristics these high-value tasks should have:

1. They should be important. These are your big-rock items—the things that your boss or customers will notice: things that will help you leave the grind behind; things that will impact your spouse, you, or other important people. Having an edge on these items will make the less-important tasks seem much more trivial and easy to deal with.

2. They should span all aspects of your life: work, family, physical, community, personal, etc. Stay in balance.

3. They should be things you've been putting off. This list will shrink in a few days). Have you been avoiding a particular phone call? Do you need to have a tough conversation with someone? Is there something big you simply need to start? What is nagging you? Add it to the list. You probably just need help to get it done. Let your subconscious help.

4. They don't need to be "completion" tasks. Perhaps you just need your subconscious to help you start something. Instead of saying "I'll write a book tomorrow," say "I'll start writing my book tomorrow and complete at least 20 pages." One of the best project managers I worked with lived and died by the phrase "kicking the ball down field." There is a lot of power in this statement. I want you to accomplish a lot, but don't expect to meet your big goals every day. Constantly moving forward is the best method I've found for maintaining exceptional productivity and momentum.

5. They should be highly complex. I can consciously figure out what 2 + 3 is. But here's the sort of problem your subconscious loves to take on: I have a highly-detailed spreadsheet, with many external references, lookups, and complex pivot tables. I cannot figure out why an equation is giving me an unexpected result. I've actively thought about it and played with it for hours. My conscious mind is stumped and has given up. My subconscious responds, "Challenge accepted." Think of your subconscious as the computer in your brain. If you give it space to do its thing, it will chug through numbers and permutations, over and over, until it comes back and delivers the answer or the guidance you need.

6. The tasks can also be creative. Your subconscious has the enviable opportunity to work distraction free. This affords it the ability to not only chug away as an efficient data processor, but also allows it to pull together

images and quotes that you've filed away over time. It will then deliver an inspirational package, ready to be turned into a work of art.

Step 3: You need to ask other people for help.

For each and every action, assign one primary person that is required to help complete the task. If you don't think anyone is needed to help you with even the smallest tasks, you're wrong. People are important in everything you do.

Who has the helpful information you need? Who is the person you've been dreading calling? Who will be happy you've completed a task? Who needs to give you time to complete it?

Visualization helps here. Visualize that person. See yourself being happy because you completed the item. See them being happy you completed it. Say thank you. See them smile in response.

By doing this, you are conditioning yourself to see that people want to help you. This will make you less afraid to ask for what you need. People like to help, but most of us don't ask. We're afraid to ask, afraid to sell. Let your subconscious get you over this nonsense.

For this step, I often pick people who have been difficult or intimidating in the past. I am often pleasantly surprised by how easy they are to deal with the next day. In reality, I'm getting my mind to abandon the pre-conception these people are difficult or intimidating. Thus, my approach to them is improved and so are the results.

Step 4: Let it go!

You should put together your list before bed. Write the tasks down. Now, close your eyes and visualize handing off the description of the desired end-state for these tasks. You should then see your subconscious leaving the room. You should know and have confidence that your subconscious will return with the completed items.

Just two final tips:

1. Your requests must be end-state oriented. That is where your subconscious excels—just like a great employee. Be able to see what you want. This is not fluff. This is your brain making the end-state so clear that you can actually see it. You can experience the feeling you'll get when your subconscious hands you the completed work. You know exactly what you want. And now your subconscious does too. The alternative is a *fuzzy request*. Fuzzy requests will give fuzzy results; just like with actual delegation.

2. Avoid the *how*. Again, just like with employee delegation, you provide a task and let them complete it. You don't map out every step they should take. *What* is the domain of the conscious; *how* is the domain of the subconscious. Your conscious mind is too tied up in day-to-day nonsense to be able to see the bigger playing field and know the right moves to make. Letting go and trusting your subconscious to figure out the *how* is key to successfully delegating tasks to your Grinder Jeeves.

Now, as any good delegator, your job is done. Have faith in your subconscious. Know that you will receive results that surpass those your active mind could produce. Don't micro-manage. Look forward to the results. Trusting the process becomes easier and easier as you see results over time.

Grinder Summary

1. There is a difference between the actively controlled part of your brain and the subconscious part.
2. Inspiration is not random; it is a mechanism afforded to your body that can be managed and leveraged.
3. Your subconscious works on problems while you're not actively thinking about them. It often produces better results.
4. Your subconscious requires clarity in order to perform. Visualization gives you clarity. The two go hand-in-hand.
5. Want to learn more? Read the best book ever written on visualization and subconscious: *Psycho Cybernetics* by
6. Maxwell Maltz, M.D., F.I.C.S.

Grinder Action: Create Your Delegate

Take the time right now to figure out whom you want to delegate tasks to. Hold a visualization session to start the iterative process of being able to see, in detail, your subconscious delegate. Make it a single person or a whole team, but either way, work on developing a strong visual and emotional sense of your new right-hand man.

Grinder Habit: Nightly Delegation

Now that you have a good understanding of visualization and delegating tasks to your subconscious, it's time to add these habits to your daily routine. Don't worry, we're nearing the end of the daily habits. I know it's a lot to do, but if you put these practices together and do them consistently, I am certain you will be absolutely amazed with the results.

In terms of a daily routine, here's exactly how I handle delegating to my subconscious. I do this before bed each night.

1. I grab a notebook and write down the 3 - 5 things I want to accomplish *tomorrow*, focusing on important, complex, and creative items.

2. I take a moment to close my eyes and identify what would happen if these tasks were complete. I imagine feeling how I will feel when they're finished.

3. I open my eyes and return to my notebook. Next to each task, I write down the name of the person I want help from.

4. I visualize the people on that list helping or congratulating me. I make them smile. I tell them "thank you."

5. Now I'm ready to delegate to my subconscious. I visualize Grinder Jeeves walking into the room. I explain what I want. I visualize describing the desired end result, but not how to get there.

6. I hear Grinder Jeeves say, "Got it, I'm on it! I'll figure how to do this and what the details are."

7. I watch as he walks out the door on a purposeful mission.

8. I now open my eyes, knowing my subconscious has a clear set of objectives for the night.

9. I go to sleep. I like to avoid adding additional clutter. My mind is cleared, so it's a great time to fall asleep. And oftentimes, I find myself falling asleep somewhere in this process. Apparently, it's good medicine to hand off what has been cluttering my mind.

Follow these steps the way I do, and when you wake up, watch for the inspiration to hit. It will hit while you're doing something else. For me, the ideas or "ah-ha" moments usually come while I'm exercising, in the shower, or driving to the office. Be prepared to stop what you're doing and jot down a few notes. It can be very easy to receive your message and promptly forget it.

It takes a little while to develop these skills, but once you do, I believe you will be amazed by the brain power you have been missing out on.

CHAPTER 8

Maximize Your Mind

Certain societies have long required memorization as a core discipline for their members. Memorization allows secret information to be passed on for generations without the risk of having written words fall into the wrong hands. But are there other reasons memorization is a cornerstone of these groups? Do they use it to provide themselves with a mental edge?

In terms of continuing to maximize what you can expect from your mind while working toward your goal of leaving the grind behind, we are going to explore two exploitable benefits of memorization:

1. Memorization exercises your brain in a unique way, helping keep you sharp longer. It can improve memory, creativity, and general mental performance.

2. If you memorize your life purpose, goals, affirmations, and visualizations, your focus on reaching them will be ratcheted to a new level. Memorization allows you to

deeply associate with your path. If someone asked you what your life purpose is, could you recite it to them word-for- word? If so, that is clarity of purpose.

I have seen incredible speeches delivered in person by some great folks. Delivering a speech with emotion, meaning, and charisma takes an incredible confluence of skills. What, however, has been most amazing to me, is that some of the speeches I watch are memorized word-for-word. As I've found, this sort of memorization is a hidden tool that can boost your brain much in the same way lifting weights can boost your muscles.

I've been fortunate enough to see people deliver these passionate speeches containing ridiculously long passages of memorized text. While this might not be the most exciting thing you can do with a free night, you cannot help but be in awe of the mental feat that's on display.

I have also been around people who do this type of memorization as part of their regular routines, treating it as exercise that is every bit important as traditional physical exercise. What is immediately apparent is that these people are *tack sharp*, regardless of age. Memorization, it would seem, is a secret weapon in the fight to maintain strong mental acuity.

Research on memorization tends to focus on its application in learning, which is not what this chapter is about. We all know memorizing facts in school is not the best way to learn.

What I'm instead talking about here is a great way to take your brain to the gym. And if you're doing something big like leaving the grind behind, don't you want to have optimal mental performance?

> "The more mental gymnastics you do, the more agile and the quicker your brain becomes."
>
> ~ Neurobiologist Nathan Tublitz ~

The Top 3 Benefits of Memorization

1. Focused minds have better creative capacity.

If you think of your mind as your office, you can begin to think about how organization relates to performing big, important tasks. If your brain is able to take in large amounts of information and then store it properly, you're better able to spend time on important tasks and less time on menial ones, such as digging through papers.

Memorization teaches your brain how to efficiently file, store, and retrieve data. Once you're organized, you can more easily create connections between disparate ideas, be creative, and leave the grind behind. Organization, therefore, allows you to spend less time being distracted and more time on higher-order thinking.

Backing this, researchers in the Netherlands found "...*working memory capacity (WMC) relates to creative performance because it enables persistent, focused, and systematic combining of elements and possibilities (persistence).*" -Sage Journals.

2. Active brain engagement and memorization keeps your brain nimble and quick.

Alright, I'll admit that one year after I moved to a new town, I still didn't know my "new" phone number by heart. But why does it matter? I can just look it up in my ever-handy mobile device!

But is it possible to stagnate and become mentally dull, thanks to our always-present mobile devices? On Christmas Eve, I went for coffee with my wife. There, we saw a family of four seated at the table. Each person had two devices: an iPhone and then either a laptop or tablet. No joke. Each had their faces buried in information, and none uttered a word the entire time we were there.

This has become the new norm for many folks, and to be frank, it's hard to pass up the allure of the immediate gratification that smartphones deliver. However, this type and quantity of information access is something very new to humans.

Not to say all surfing is mindless, but it's easy to find yourself zoned out in a state of information overload, thumbing through social gossip. In this state, you begin to find it difficult to connect to other humans. You feel dull. You're turning your mind away from the present and losing your ability to be quick, nimble, and engaged.With this in mind, I urge you to unplug and take your brain out for some mental exercise. UCLA neuroscientist Arthur Toga points out that *"any reading, which requires a sequence of tasks in the brain, 'gets a lot more circuits involved' than simply watching* television." He further states *"that it is 'use-it-or-lose-it' when it comes to brain function over time."*

If you're spending your time watching TV and surfing low-value topics on the Internet, you're training your brain in a very specific way that does not enable your goal to leave the grind behind.

If instead you train your brain to better store and retrieve information on the fly, you will stand out and be suited for the skills required of a future Grinder.

> **"Whenever you squander attention on something that doesn't put your brain through its paces and stimulate change, your mind stagnates a little and life feels dull."**
>
> **~ Winifred Gallagher, Rapt ~**

3. Memorization teaches your brain how to recall information.

Much like physical training, mental training requires *specificity*. By practicing memorization, you become better at efficiently remembering and recalling information. This is a well-researched topic, and something succinctly described in a paper published by Lumos Labs, Inc, San Francisco State University, and Stanford University in the paper *Enhancing Visual Attention and Working Memory*:

"Until relatively recently, the conventional wisdom in the neuroscience and cognitive science communities held that cognitive capacity was essentially fixed after a relatively brief critical period of

early development. However, we now know that the adult brain— rather than being a fixed-capacity machine—is an adaptable, plastic organ capable of continual improvement in efficiency and effectiveness when exposed to the proper experiences. It has been demonstrated that the human brain's inherent plasticity allows for the improvement, via targeted training exercises, of cognitive skills involving aspects of speed of processing, attention, working memory, and fluid intelligence."

In and of itself, this is worthy of the practice time. Your ability to think on your feet, perform your job well, and interact with people, is largely based on being able to recall interesting, topical, and important information. Memorization training allows you to improve and maintain your brain's recollective power.

I'm Convinced! What Should I Memorize?

Here are some great memorization techniques to get you going.

Memorize poems

This is probably the most commonly recommended method you'll see. And you'll be in company that dates back to 500 BC, when Pythagoras and his followers exercised their memories abundantly, leveraging poetry as a primary tool.

Poems have nice cadence, catchy rhyming, and other tools that assist the memorization process. They are a great bridge to moving on to more complicated forms of text memorization as well.

Now that you know about this secret weapon, be wary the person who walks around with a small book of poems in their pocket.

"There is something to be gained from memorizing great literature, like poetry, or from great speeches from history. Why? Because one is learning to speak eloquently, and one can draw on that knowledge when it comes to one's own self-expression."

~ Howard Gardner of the Harvard Graduate School of Education ~

Play an instrument

Memorization is a huge component of playing a musical instrument, whether piano, guitar, or something else. As with poems, you'll have many other aspects than just the raw notes to help make the memorization easier.

Plus, research has shown that the more parts of your brain you engage, the better the results of the mental activity. Playing music requires physical coordination, reading, memorization, listening, and so many other aspects. I can hardly think of a better way to engage the mind.

Playing an instrument affords an exceptional additional benefit, as well. As you already learned in this book, leveraging your subconscious is your tool for solving complex problems. Often, the problem is tricking your conscious into "letting go" and getting out of the way. Playing an instrument absorbs you and your conscious efforts. It gives your subconscious space to play, and therefore, your creative energy realizes a boost.

Well, I bet you didn't expect to see "play an instrument" in a book about quitting your job to start on your own path to greatness. But there are strong secondary benefits from it, so get on it.

Grinder Summary

1. Take your brain to the gym using memorization.
2. Since you can now have Google in your hand anytime and anywhere, the regular application of memory is becoming less commonplace. Don't let your brain become a victim.
3. Memorization has the following bottom-line benefits:
   a. Focused minds have better capacity for creativity.
   b. Be more interesting.
   c. Active brain engagement and memorization keeps your brain nimble and quick.
   d. Memorization teaches your brain how to recall information.
4. Jumpstart your memorization training by memorizing poems or playing a musical instrument.

Grinder Action: Memorize Your Goals and Affirmations

By following the other Grinder Actions in this book, you are naturally learning the process of memorization. Many of the routines in this book are performed at least once per day and involve writing. By consistently engaging both your mind and body, you are learning memorization.

In fact, that's why these routines are so effective. You are burning both your goals and supporting beliefs into your brain. Your image of success is becoming an increasingly comfortable tenant in your head.

To really confirm your brain is on task, memorize your life purpose, GRINDER 3 goals, and top 3 affirmations. Try reading them aloud from cards. Then, try looking at yourself in the mirror and repeating them. Commit these to memory, word-for-word.

Grinder Habit: Replace Reading with Recitation

Once you have your life purpose, GRINDER 3 goals, and top 3 affirmations memorized, you can skip reading them. Instead recite them to yourself out loud—preferably while looking at yourself in a mirror.

To be clear, I do not want you to replace any written exercises. It's key to engage physically in this process too. But you should replace reading with recitation.

SECTON 1

Summary

We have covered a lot of ground in this section. The mental tactics covered are critical to your goal of leaving the grind behind, but they have much broader applications as well. If you commit to these practices, I fully expect you will see your life quickly improve across the board.

So how do you take this information and make it an actual habit? Daily tracking. Success is in the daily habits.

Go now to **grindbehindbook.com/tools**. There, you'll find a weekly worksheet. You'll use it to write down your GRINDER 3 and check off your daily actions as they're done.

Even though I've been doing this stuff for years, I still use daily action trackers. It's that important.

You can see a sample from the tracker on the next page.

Weekly Grinder Habit Tracker

Instructions:
1. Print this sheet off once per week and fill it out by hand before starting your week.
2. Refer to the chapter numbers referenced for additional instruction and guidance.
3. Place a check in the daily boxes as you complete items.
4. Keep motivated at GrindBehindBook.com

Ch 3	My life purpose is:	
Ch 4	My GRINDER Goal 1 is:	
Ch 4	My GRINDER Goal 2 is:	
Ch 4	My GRINDER Goal 3 is:	
Ch 5	My #1 Affirmation is:	
Ch 5	My #2 Affirmation is:	
Ch 5	My #3 Affirmation is:	

	Mindset Habits	Sun	Mon	Tues	Weds	Thurs	Fri	Sat
Ch 2	Write down 5 positive things from today							
Ch 2	Write down 5 positive things you look forward to tomorrow							
Ch 3	Review of your life purpose upon waking							
Ch 4	Review your GRINDER 3 goals in the morning							
Ch 4	Review your GRINDER 3 affirmations throughout the day							
Ch 6	Visualize successful completion of your GRINDER 3							
Ch 7	At bedtime, delegate 2 to 5 tasks to your subconscous							

grindbehindbook.com/tools

Alight, now that you have a basis, it's time to move to the nuts-and-bolts of your goal to leave the grind behind.

SECTION 2

The Grinder's Network

SECTION 2 INTRODUCTION:

The Grinder's Network

It's not what you know; it's who you know. We've all heard this saying, and if you want to leave the grind behind, you'll need to live and breathe it. Even though this concept applies to the Cog world, it applies doubly so to the Grinder world.

Humans progress because we learn and advance from those that came before. Grinders know this and don't re-invent the wheel. You have the ability to level-jump results, avoid pitfalls, and leverage others' connections.

This section will explain:

1. How to create a personal board of directors.
2. How to find a great mentor.

I'm an introvert by nature, so I can assure you this section is not about going door-to-door or making cold calls. This is about smartly and meaningfully connecting with your network. And I assure you that if you apply the principles in this section, you'll build a massive safety net that will help you break ties with the grind.

Though Section 2 is short, it's massively important. It is a prerequisite for taking the real-world action in Section 3.

CHAPTER 9

The Grinder's Board of Directors

Like the chapter on GRINDER 3 goals, this is a pivotal chapter. The actions here will be referenced throughout the remaining chapters. So buckle up. You're about to build a group dedicated to helping you leave the grind behind.

Having a trusted team will greatly improve your chances of success, help you over hurdles, and keep you from slacking. Think about it...at work, you typically tackle big goals in a team. Personal goals are no different. You'll achieve more with the help of a team that is focused on your success.

So get ready to create your own personal board of directors— your own Mastermind Group. Yes, this is the concept Napoleon Hill helped make massively popular, which is:

"Coordination of knowledge and effort, in a spirit of harmony, between two or more people, for the attainment of a definite purpose."

~ Napoleon Hill, Think and Grow Rich ~

Having a group to provide outside perspective, tools, and motivation to bring each other's' success to another level is something many successful people throughout history have done. The value is undeniable.

"During a newspaper interview with the great steel magnate, I asked him (Andrew Carnegie) to what he attributed his success. He replied by asking me to define the term success. When I told him I had reference to his money, he said: 'Well, if you want to know how I got my money, I will refer you to these men here on my staff; they got it for me. We have here in this business a master mind. It is not my mind, and it is not the mind of any other man on my staff, but the sum of all these minds that I have gathered around me that constitute a master mind in the steel business.'"

~ Napoleon Hill, Think and Grow Rich ~

Before diving in, I want to caution that the term Mastermind Group has become fairly trendy. Much like with affirmations, people are misusing and diluting the value of the concept.

Indeed, there are many products for sale that tout a Mastermind Group as a benefit. Others directly charge you monthly to be part of their Mastermind Group. These groups typically meet in a private Facebook Page or similar online chats.

These are *not* effective Mastermind Group constructs. If you are in one of these, do not skip this chapter. You likely are not gaining the true benefit of being in a Mastermind Group. Avoid preconceptions and stick to what I describe here.

9 Characteristics of a True Mastermind Group

A Mastermind Group is an assembly of success-oriented people. These individuals are seeking to make big changes in their lives. All work together to drive joint improvement and accountability.

Here are the 9 foundational characteristics of Mastermind Groups that are most beneficial:

1. Weekly cadence

This helps keep everyone fresh and isn't overwhelming. Meet once per week for one hour. Get together with a few trusted people on a consistent basis, either in-person, by conference call, or video...but *not* by ad-hoc chat or messaging. Have a recurring meeting on the calendar.

2. Group purpose

Determine an underlying reason for having the group. This ensures the group doesn't stray off track. I recommend a tagline like: *To use the synergy of its group members in order to accelerate the realization of each member's GRINDER 3 goals.*

3. Individual goals

Identify each individual's goals and reasons for being in the group. What do you want the group to help you achieve? These goals are ones that you believe are bigger than you can achieve on your own. Typically, these goals will be your GRINDER 3.

4. Weekly Actions

Each week, each member tells the group which activities they will work on in the upcoming week. Each member should list 3-5 activities they want to have accomplished by next session.

5. Accountability

Each week, each member tells the group whether they achieved last week's activities. This is a huge benefit of a Mastermind Group. Suddenly, you're accountable to people other than yourself. This is motivational and keeps you from slacking.

Those goals you committed to last week? This week, you get to stand up in front of the group and cover your progress.

6. Individual focus

On a rotational basis, each member gets the floor. During this time, you remind the group what your goals are, how you're progressing, and discuss where you need help.

This gives everyone else the opportunity to see the scope of each other's goals. You get to offer thoughts, advice, and tips, which opens your eyes to ideas you may not have seen yourself.

I generally recommend that one person takes the floor each week. This is really where most of the magic happens. I have learned so much by letting other people dissect my goals and how I'm achieving them. Perhaps someone in your group has a contact that will help you achieve your goal. Or, perhaps they've already made the mistake you're about to make. The possibilities are wide open.

7. Encouraging and critical

Do your part as a member by helping other members as much as they're helping you. Give the positive encouragement they need. But don't be shy to highlight information they may be overlooking, areas in which they may not be shooting high enough, or goals they should consider adding.

8. Self-reflection

Another great part of a Mastermind Group is you can often see in others what you can't see in yourself. For example, I have seen people who spend way too much time at work and not enough on personal pursuits. As a result, I reflected and realized I was in the same boat. This sort of reflective analysis makes you look harder at yourself and helps you determine whether or not you're truly on track. It's easier to see flaws in others.

9. Simple and free

How much does this terrific construct cost you? Nothing. You're getting enormous benefit without shelling out any dough. Can't beat that.

Keep the meetings simple, too. All you really need is a phone with a conference button or something like Skype.

Once you're in a rhythm with your group, I can practically guarantee you'll start speeding toward your goals.

Mastermind Rules for Outstanding Results

As you begin running your group, you'll want to establish certain rules to ensure consistency and success. I'll provide you the three rules I use in my groups. These should ratchet up everyone's results.

You may consider reviewing these rules with the group at the start of each session, while also layering in your own rules to complement your particular group's dynamic.

1. Treat your group as your personal board of directors

The best way to look at your grind-bucking journey is to consider yourself the CEO of your life. Just like any good CEO, you want to grow and improve your business until it's an epic, thriving entity. CEOs don't run wild though; they must report to the board of directors.

Once a month in your Mastermind Group, you take the hot seat. You are the CEO of your life. The other members in your group act as your personal board of directors. This analogy is a very powerful way to approach how you discuss your goals and performance with the group.

To formalize this, have a running presentation that covers:

1. Your vision.
2. Your GRINDER 3 goals.
3. Graphs that demonstrate each goal's actual versus target.
4. Plans to achieve your goals.
5. Where you need help.

As your board of directors listens, expect them to engage and do the following:

1. Broaden and refine your vision, ensuring it covers all aspects of life.
2. Point out when you're off course.
3. Refine your goals and ensure they are big enough (often, groups are more ambitious than individuals).
4. Help with your plan. They may highlight opportunities, offering to introduce you to someone or by providing direction based on their experience.
5. Provide general support, increasing the believability and likelihood of achieving your large goals. Remember those mental hacks from Section 1?

"You'll find that when you share your vision, some people will want to help you make it happen. Others will introduce you to friends and resources that can help you.

You'll also find that each time that you share your vision, it becomes clearer and feels more real and attainable. And most importantly, every time you share your vision, you strengthen your own subconscious belief that you can achieve it."

~ Jack Canfield, The Success Principles ~

2. Provide support and belief

It is amazing what you can accomplish when other people support and believe in you. It's even more amazing what you accomplish when you believe in yourself and your ability to accomplish big goals.

"The number one problem that keeps people from winning in the United States today is lack of belief in themselves."

~ Arthur L Williams ~

Initially, it can be surprisingly difficult to tell other people your big goals, your life purpose, and what your dream life looks like. This is a symptom of you not fully believing in yourself. Perhaps you're embarrassed at some level, don't believe you can do it, or have been derided by others for dreaming big.

A commitment to sincerely following rule #2 will fuel a Mastermind Group's synergistic magic.

3. Commit...Commit...Commit

If you want results from your Mastermind Group, you need to be all in. You need to commit. Commit to yourself that you will take your journey seriously. Commit to the rest of the group that you will actively listen, support, and help them achieve their goals. Commit the time. It doesn't take much.

These seem like easy things to do, but if the team isn't committed, it won't excel.

Ultimately, if this is not time you're excited for, you may be with the wrong group of people. You should enjoy spending this time immensely. You should see how it fuels your life.

Grinder
Summary

1. Mastermind Group is a group of success-oriented people trying to make big changes in their lives, all working together to drive joint improvement and accountability

2. Private chat and Facebook groups have become mediums trendy marketers use to sell alleged Mastermind Groups. These are *not* effective Mastermind Group constructs.

3. Mastermind Groups are characterized by 9 traits:
    a. Weekly cadence
    b. Group purpose

    c. Individual goals

    d. Actions each week

    e. Accountability

    f. Individual focus

    g. Encouraging and critical

    h. Self-reflection

    i. Simple and free

4. There are three tenants for achieving outstanding Mastermind Group results. Customize these to match the dynamic of your group.

5. Treat your group like your personal board of directors.

6. Provide support and belief.

7. Commit, Commit, Commit.

Grinder Action: Form a Mastermind Group

You're ready to start. Take action. If you don't have a group of people helping you improve yourself and achieve your goals, get started.

It may be as simple as asking a couple of friends if they want to meet once per week. Over time, you can worry about diversifying your group, getting the right format, and hammering out all of the other details that may stop you from getting started.

This is a Grinder Action. Take a step forward and worry about the details later.

Grinder Habit:
Hold Regular Meetings

Once you've determined the members in your Mastermind Group, start meeting weekly. Follow the characteristics and rules outlined in this chapter. Get in the habit of regularly meeting with people about success, and success will undoubtedly follow.

CHAPTER 10

Grinder Mentors

Seeing great people in action will level-jump your results and change your perception of what's possible. In the previous chapter, you took it upon yourself to set up a Mastermind Group that acts as your board of directors. This group provides perspective and drives your success. But you'll want even more people power.

Specifically, you want a mentor. A mentor is distinct from the Mastermind Group, yet complimentary. A mentor will push your results to the next level and help you create a massive safety net for that day you leap from your Cog job.

Indeed, mentors have been instrumental in my successful departure from The Grind. If there was a milestone in my career, there was a mentor behind it.

Mentors have been down the path you're headed. They can give you directions. They can warn you of dangers. They can direct you to the shortcuts.

While Mastermind Groups can be set up fairly easily with peers in your existing network, finding the right type of mentor can be a bit more challenging. But, it is worth it. A great mentor will provide a deeper sort of relationship and may be a deciding factor for leaving the grind behind.

If you're about to make a big, risky change in your life, why not learn—hands on—from the best?

Mentors are Your Network's Turbo Charger

I have had a string of mentors throughout my career. These people have opened the door and helped me leave the grind behind. And yours will do the same for you. You just need to ask. Here's your overview of mentoring.

What mentoring means to a Grinder

Have you seen someone who excels in your desired field? Do you know someone who has repeated success in whatever they do?

Now, would your life improve if those types of people were involved in your grind-behind journey? Absolutely.

Having a mentor is one of the most rewarding activities you can engage in. To a Grinder, receiving mentoring means:

- Finding someone who has success in the areas you're interested in.
- Allowing them to tell you how they became successful, including the ups and downs.

- Reducing your risk by having them review your plans, brainstorm with you, and open doors.

Successful people want to mentor

Before asking anyone to mentor you, it's best to get your mindset right. You may think successful people are too busy and consumed in their own lives that they don't have time to mentor.

Surprisingly, people generally love to teach and love to know that their particular skills, background, and results are being noticed. I have been constantly impressed with how willing people are to take time out of their day to mentor.

This about it this way: being asked to mentor is one of the highest compliments a person can receive. You are effectively saying they have achieved what you're dreaming of.

Thought in this way, at a minimum, you will make that person smile. At best, you'll have yourself a life-changing mentor. So don't be shy about asking. It's win-win.

If you don't see mentoring in this way and don't feel comfortable asking, I recommend reading *How to Win Friends and Influence People* by Dale Carnegie.

The Mentor Relationship

You and your mentor will commit both your time and minds to the process. It's important that you take mentoring very seriously and respect your mentor's time and experience.

What your mentor deserves from you

If you are asking a successful person to take time out of their life to help you, here's what you should, at minimum, plan to do in return:

1. Listen

This goes without saying, but I like to completely disconnect from the rest of the world during my sessions. This means I turn off my phone, step away from the computer, and give my mentor full attention.

Eliminate distractions. Nothing will end a mentoring relationship faster than your inattention.

2. Ask questions

Learn how to ask leading questions and ensure the sessions are interactive. Many high-potential mentors may not yet know how to be a great mentor. Come up with a list of questions and hurdles from your current situation, but also make sure to ask questions about their life. Be prepared. Don't slack.

3. Meet on their terms and set the next appointment

Can they make time once per month over lunch? Great. Take it. Can they talk by phone at 7 p.m. once per week? Take that instead.

Make it as convenient as possible for your mentor. Also, make sure you proactively set up the next session. This shows you are excited and benefitting from the meetings.

4. Keep an open mind

One of the most important things I've learned during my mentoring sessions is that *I don't know jack.* Success comes in many forms, and it is incredible what some people credit their success to. Just because it doesn't fit your particular perspective doesn't mean it is invalid.

This one was tough for me. I'm very skeptical by nature, yet a lot of the themes that came up in my mentoring sessions were spiritual or metaphysical in nature—take Napoleon Hill's work, for example.

This did not fit into my world view at all. I wrote these ideas off for a while, but after seeing them come up repeatedly, I started taking a deeper look. This allowed me to uncover the science behind their effectiveness and put the ideas into practice.

Mentors also opened me up to the importance of having a positive attitude and leveraging my subconscious. Obviously, those suggestions have made a huge impact in my life and ended up being a major focus of this book. Good thing I let down my guard.

5. Take action

If a mentor is dedicating a good amount of their time to give life and career advice, you should show *actual application.* Put into practice what makes sense for you, but don't sit idle.

Nothing will be more satisfying for both of you than seeing actual real world results. And results won't come without action.

6. Offer your loyalty, and if needed, help

Does your mentor have something you can assist with? Offer to help. Maybe it's as simple as shoveling snow one morning. Maybe your mentor could use help with a charitable event they're running. Perhaps their business could benefit from a skill you have.

Mentors generally won't expect anything in return, but showing your appreciation can go a long way.

What you should expect from your mentor

Mentors are all different. Some people are more adept at analyzing their own lives and teaching than others.

While you should help facilitate and ask questions, also allow the mentor to play to their own strengths. This is the best way to observe this person in their true state, which is what you're looking for. If the mentor is trying to cater to a specific expectation, you won't get what you need.

- Ultimately, a good mentor will:
- Tell you their story
- Help apply their learnings to your journey.
- Hold you accountable.
- Provide motivation.
- Link you to their network.

Who should you ask to be your mentor?

Now that you have an idea of what happens with a mentor, it's time to find one. But going on this hunt can seem daunting.

In order to simplify the search process, I start by targeting certain types of people. Here are a few of the types I recommend you hone in on:

1. Your boss

If you choose to approach your boss, say you admire their accomplishments. And be specific. Ask them to mentor you "off the clock." I guarantee that boss will see you differently.

And since your boss is in a higher position than you, it's likely have something to learn. If you then start turning these sessions into positive action, you will make both yourself and your boss look awesome.

2. Your boss's boss

This is, perhaps, my favorite. It's similar to #1, but much more powerful. You may be surprised, but I have never had my boss's boss say *no* to a mentor request.

The stakes are a little higher here, so you need to take your side of the responsibility seriously (re-read "What your mentor deserves from you").

Often, the higher your mentor is up the chain, the closer they will be to behaving like a Grinder. These people can probably better prepare you for life after the grind. Plus, if you impress your boss's boss with questions, informed flattery, and action, only good will come from it.

3. Someone who "has it all"

Do you know someone who always has time for their family, enjoys a lot of leisure time, and makes money hand-over-fist? Most of us have a thoroughbred Grinder in our extended network.

If this person generally has a very successful, well-balanced life, it's very likely they'll be interested in helping others. In fact, helping you will probably fall right into their plan.

The trick to this one is the approach. Ensure your story is well crafted. Have everything complete from Section 1 of this book. Be clear about what you want, what your purpose is, and what your goals are. Use this as a basis for the discussion.

4. Someone who provides you services

Does your life insurance agent wear a Rolex and drive a Mercedes? Mine does. He's happy too. Can I learn something from him? Yep.

But here's why this one wins—he will see it as a way to deepen your relationship, thereby making you a lifelong customer.

To be clear, I'm not recommending you ask just anybody to be your mentor. Find someone who provides you a service through a company they partially own or for which they are largely responsible. You want someone who is a Grinder or is close to being one.

5. A consultative customer

Once you're at the cusp of leaving the grind behind, it's time to seek out people who can use your expertise in a consultative capacity.

If they are successful and doing something big, they will probably need some form of assistance. Figure out how you can exchange your expertise for mentoring.

Apart from just mentoring, you'll gain the ability to be present and involved with someone who has already left the grind behind. Hugely valuable exposure.

To this day, I still offer my services at a discount to the right people who are willing to let me in on how they operate. It's win-win.

6. Someone in your social club, association, or society

Many people belong to social or community groups. If you don't, it's a great way to quickly expand your network. This might be a church, society, volunteer organization, or country club. Joining an organization like this can be free or carry a fee. Regardless of what it is, I highly recommend you find an organization to plug into.

Once you get to know the members, think about which can help you. Since members share a common bond, the transition to a deeper relationship is easy.

The 3 important qualities of a mentor

As you begin identifying candidates, you can narrow down your list by looking for three particular qualities.

Quality 1: Have they already achieved what you are looking to achieve?

This may seem fairly obvious, but it requires a bit of homework. Starting where someone else has already been is really key to getting anywhere in life quickly, safely, and with minimal hassle. Human progress is based on this principle.

Build on other people's success; don't start from scratch. You accomplish this by finding the right person, learning their model, trusting the model, implementing it, and adjusting as you go.

To put this into real terms, if you decide you want to write a book, find someone in your network who has written a book. Better yet, find someone who has successfully sold many books.

If you want to be a millionaire, look for someone who is already a millionaire. It's that easy. Do you want to achieve some goal no one ever has before? Well, you're still in luck—look for people who have done something new. These pioneers can be your guide.

Quality 2: Have they failed at times yet achieved your goal several times over?

What's even better than a one-time success? Someone who failed along the way, powered through, and then continued to achieve success again and again. Maybe they've hit their goal, lost everything, and then amazingly hit it again.

Failure is a learning opportunity…nothing more, nothing less. By having a mentor, you simply get to learn from mistakes faster and with less pain.

You're not just looking for failures here. Also look for people who have simply accomplished your goal multiple times in multiple ways. If you want to own a rental home, someone who has purchased 100 rentals is probably a better resource than someone who has purchased one.

Quality 3: Did they achieve your goal with a compatible set of values and ethics?

This quality is a surprisingly important part of this qualification process. You need to figure out if people accomplished your goal with a set of values that match yours.

If not, you will not follow their model. You may even begin to believe you can't accomplish your goals, because only people with x, y, or z attributes can accomplish the goal.

I'll give a personal example. Here's a list of my personal goals and values:

1. Attain a specific large net worth
2. Have a specific large annual income

3. Be in business for myself

4. Spend plenty of time with my family

5. Be highly interested in how I spend my time

6. Be charitable and give back

7. Be able to look back at my one-and-only life and be happy about how I spent it

8. Venture through all areas of my life with honesty and integrity

So should I find a mentor that makes a ton of money but travels 90% of the time in order to do so? No. That would be dangerous for me. It might make me believe I won't be able to get what I want because I'm unwilling to be constantly away from my family.

Values are key to living happily. If you to listen to people who have accomplished your goal, but don't mesh with your values, then you are reinforcing incorrect beliefs.

This will make you less likely to achieve your goals than if you hadn't listened to that person in the first place. Failing to evaluate your values and find mentors with similar values can be very detrimental to your ability to achieve or even start a goal.

The Indirect Benefits of Asking Someone to Mentor

Apart from spending time with successful people, learning great keys to success, and building your own vision for success, there are some surprising fringe benefits of having a mentor.

1. Mentors generally become your champions...and hopefully your customers

If you're leaving the grind behind, you need all the champions and customers you can get. Successful people have excellent people networks. If you're doing your part, your mentor will be invested in your success and will advertise for you: "Hey, I know this great guy who can help you out with…"

2. Mentors will open doors to success for you

Your mentor will want to see you apply their teachings and succeed while doing so. Because of this, they will likely pull extra strings to make things happen.

Some of my best contacts are those that have mentored me. They've let me know about excellent opportunities and vouched for my capabilities. Most of my promotions and other career milestones have their roots in one of my mentors.

3. Mentors will give you their secrets...and buy you lunch

When I first started working in real estate, I asked one of the top performing agents in the office if I could take him to lunch and pick his brain a bit. He was happy to do so and gave me some wonderful advice. Once lunch wrapped up, he insisted on paying.

The next day, at the office meeting, he jokingly said, "Watch out for Justin. I took him out to lunch yesterday and gave him all of my secrets."

Another agent responded, "Wow. He talked you into handing over all of your secrets and buying lunch? You're right—I will watch out for him."

The point is, people are proud to impart their knowledge and will give you much more than you expect.

4. You will build easier working relationships and lifelong, loyal friends

There is something fairly intimate about the mentoring relationship. Each person is sharing deep parts of their life. You're both being introspective. You're both rooting for each other's ongoing success. This is a very unique bond.

5. The biggie—risk reduction

As we all undoubtedly know, leaving the grind behind is risky. If you're the sole-supporter of a family along with numerous financial obligations, it is doubly so. But that risk is manageable, thanks in large part to mentors.

If you want to successfully leave the grind behind, there's no reason to re-invent the wheel every step of the way. Find shortcuts and avoid pitfalls by spending time with people who have been there, done that. That's what I mean by *standing on the shoulders of greats*.

Should You Pay for a Mentor?

The people who have made the biggest difference in my life have been people who have chosen to mentor me out of their personal desire to help others. However, I haven't always been able to find just the right mentor. In some cases, it made sense for me to use professional programs.

There are, in fact, many professional coaching programs out there for pretty much any line of business.

The quality can vary, but on the upside, there are long-standing programs that are staffed with top players looking to add mentoring to their portfolio. People typically love to teach and coach, so this becomes a natural progression for fantastic careers.

If you're not able to get what you need from a mentor within your network, I certainly recommend exploring paid coaching programs. While they can be expensive, I've had very good overall luck and fully believe they've paid for themselves several times over. That's not to say all of my paid coaches have been perfect.

Ultimately, a paid program really needs to get you out of your comfort zone, challenge and criticize your current path, and kick your goals into action. Most programs have multiple coaches, one of whom will be assigned to you. I like to see a structured system in place to ensure, regardless of the coach assigned, my experience will be consistent.

To summarize, paying for a mentor is not necessarily a bad thing. If you are having a hard time finding someone within your network to act as a mentor, or you are targeting a very specific niche, it may make sense for you to go for a paid program. As you and your business grow, it will make more and more sense for you to regularly engage a paid coach.

Grinder
Summary

1. Don't be shy about asking someone to mentor you. It's generally a win-win.

2. Here are the behaviors and responsibilities you owe your mentor:

    a. Listen

    b. Ask questions

    c. Meet on their terms and set the next appointment d. Keep an open mind

    d. Take action

    e. Give them your loyalty and help

3. Here are your great potential mentors:

    a. Your boss

    b. Your boss's boss

    c. Someone who "has it all"

    d. Someone who provides you services e. A consultative customer

4. Validate your mentors against the qualities identified in this chapter, including:

    a. Have they succeeded where you want to succeed?

    b. Have they repeatedly failed and succeeded?

    c. Do their values match yours?

5. Having a mentor is one of the most important ingredients in risk reduction.

6. If you are living up to your side of the mentoring relationship, your mentor will want you to succeed. They'll want their trusted network involved in higher levels of your business.

7. Read How to Win Friends and Influence People by Dale Carnegie.

Grinder Action:
List 10 Possible Mentors

To get the ball rolling, start a list of 10 potential mentors, choosing a few from each of the categories mentioned in this chapter. If you can list more, great.

For each, do the following:

1. Write down what they could do to improve your chances of achieving your GRINDER 3.

2. Research their business and professional life to see what their opportunities and challenges are. Jot down a few notes so you can have a more insightful conversation during a first meeting.

3. Hold a brief visualization session for each in which you imagine seeing them being glad to see you. See them reach out, shake your hand, give you a big smile. This is how mentors will receive you; just make sure you believe it.

Grinder Habit: Work Your List Daily

Until you have an active mentor you're meeting with on a regular basis, you need to keep working until you find one. So— as it goes with tough tasks—make sure to just take consistent action. Soon enough, you'll have what you want.

Make it a point to take an action once per day toward the goal of having a mentor. This action might involve defining your list, calling someone from the list, or revising the list. If your list ends up full of dead ends, consult your Mastermind Group for help.

Once you've locked in a mentor, start meeting regularly, and make sure you initiate the meetings. To reach the depth of value you'll need from your mentor, this should be an ongoing, monthly, evolving relationship.

SECTION 2

Summary

As you work toward becoming a Grinder, you can drastically improve your chances of leaving the grind behind, while also reducing the risk of doing so, if you plug the right people in. They will support you, open doors, help you avoid mistakes, and welcome you into their network.

Here's how you can best leverage your network:

1. Team up with like-minded people who will become your own personal board of directors. If you haven't already set up a Mastermind Group, get to it. This is a pre-requisite for Section 3.
2. Seek out a mentor.
3. Read How to Win Friends and Influence People by Dale Carnegie.

In this section, you've also picked up new actions you need to be taking on a regular basis. If you haven't already, go now to **grindbehindbook.com/tools**. There, you'll find a weekly worksheet to print out. It includes tracking tools to that will keep you on the path to building a Grinder-worthy network. See the full version of the tracker below.

Weekly Grinder Habit Tracker

Instructions:
1. Print this sheet off once per week and fill it out by hand before starting your week.
2. Refer to the chapter numbers referenced for additional instruction and guidance.
3. Place a check in the daily boxes as you complete items.
4. Keep motivated at grindbehindbook.com

Ch 3	My life purpose is:	
Ch 4	My GRINDER Goal 1 is:	
Ch 4	My GRINDER Goal 2 is:	
Ch 4	My GRINDER Goal 3 is:	
Ch 5	My #1 Affirmation is:	
Ch 5	My #2 Affirmation is:	
Ch 5	My #3 Affirmation is:	

	Mindset Habits	Sun	Mon	Tues	Weds	Thurs	Fri	Sat
Ch 2	Write down 5 positive things from today							
Ch 2	Write down 5 positive things you look forward to tomorrow							
Ch 3	Review of your life purpose upon waking							
Ch 4	Review your GRINDER 3 goals in the morning							
Ch 4	Review your GRINDER 3 affirmations throughout the day							
Ch 6	Visualize successful completion of your GRINDER 3							
Ch 7	At bedtime, delegate 3 to 5 tasks to your subconscious							

	Network & Action	Sun	Mon	Tues	Weds	Thurs	Fri	Sat
Ch 9	I met with my Mastermind Group this week							
Ch 10	I have a meeting scheduled with my mentor this month							
Ch 11	I am uncomfortable with my job, which means I am growing							
Ch 12	I wrote down my tasks for the day and used the Pomodoro Technique							
Ch 13	I took at least one action on each of my GRINDER 3 today							

grindbehindbook.com/tools

SECTION 3

The Grinder's Actions

SECTION 3 INTRODUCTION:

The Grinder's Actions

Now that you've completed Sections 1 and 2, you're ready for the truth: you have everything you need to leave the grind behind, and by doing so, create a grind that works for you.

There are countless people who have become Grinders with nothing more than the right mindset and the right people. And there are millions of opportunities for you to make money on your own.

But I don't want to just say that. I want to provide you with actionable items for you to take forward. That's what Section 3 is all about. This section gives you practical tips to help actually convert your energy into action. It will cover new ways to think about money. And I will give you my thoughts on several ways to get started as a Grinder. Consider this section a Mastermind Group with me.

Now, you may think my ideas are rubbish or don't apply to you. I have no problem with that. But if they don't get you thinking and brainstorming ideas that fit your situation, that's a problem.

Indeed, this section will likely leave you with more questions than answers, which is good. I hope to stir your creative juices. Get to discussing things with your Mastermind Group. And if you'd like to bounce ideas off me and drill down into these concepts, email me at justin@grindbehindbook.com.

CHAPTER 11

Maximize Now

It's tough to quit your job and take off on something adventurous and exciting. But you can do a surprising amount in your current situation to prepare for the moment you leap.

So realize the positives in your current situation and get the most from it before quitting.

In other words—if you're not sure what you want to leave the grind for, don't sit idle. Use your time and current job to develop valuable expertise and connections (safety nets).

Leaping from Cog to Grinder

Even though I always knew I wanted to quit working in a standard environment and become a Grinder, the reality was I had *no idea* how I was going to make money on my own.

While I worked through this challenge using the mental concepts in Section 1, I also focused on the practical side by gaining everything I could from my Cog job.

Are you maximizing your time in your Cog job? There is one question to ask yourself to determine this: *am I comfortable or uncomfortable?*

Personally, I knew I was on the right Grinder trajectory if I felt:

- Unprepared.
- In over my head.
- To all external appearances, unfit and unqualified.

These feelings are a good barometer for whether or not you're expanding your comfort zone, learning, and focusing on self-improvement.

Too many people feel their job isn't good enough for them. So, do they do their best at it anyway? No…they slack off and don't commit—after all, the job is "below them." *This is a terrible approach,* and it has "Cog" written all over it. This is no way to learn, improve, or expand.

Rather, if you are not where you want to be at a company—whether entry-level or VP—put your positive mindset to work and get everything you can out of it. In general, if you approach your job as a way to grow, learn, and experiment, you will end up helping your company and yourself. You will be on the Grinder fast track.

Others in my network who have built big companies also employed these principles. All wanted to go off on their own earlier, but their time in the corporate world wasn't in vain. It helped them gain knowledge and maturity that ended up providing a big boost to their success.

8 Steps to Maximize Now

1. Get a job at a big company, even if it needs to be a lower-level position.

Working at a big company is fundamental to many of the tips you'll see in this chapter. Small companies offer great experiences too, but you'll have fewer opportunities and people to learn from. And after all, this is about networking, so you need broader exposure.

If you're a Cog and are not sure what you'll do once you quit, seek a job at a big company. Even if you have to start at a lower position than you may want, worry not and read on.

I will also add the caveat that you'll want to work in a central office location. Get in a big company and work where the action is.

2. Work hard at your job, even if it sucks or you think it's below you.

Out of college, I worked as an entry-level call center agent. Despite my past experience and a four-year degree, there just weren't many options for me. I felt overqualified and deflated, but I worked hard nevertheless.

If you don't give it your all, you won't connect with the right people. No one will open doors for you. You will lose your edge. You will cement yourself as a Cog.

So how do you work hard in a way that allows you to also gain traction for leaving the grind behind? Work hard in a smart way. To work hard smartly, figure out the metrics your boss cares about and put everything you have into those. Other tasks are low priority.

As soon as you post top results with your own work, you'll become a natural leader among your peers. If your actions boost the results of your entire team, the right people in the company will take notice. So if you want a better job, do the one you have better.

For a great example, read up on Walmart CEO Doug McMillon. His start? Loading trucks in Walmart's distribution center. He later climbed to assistant manager and then quickly up the chain to the top of Fortune 500's #1 company (as of 2015).

3. Tell your boss you want as much experience as possible so that you can quit. Tell your boss' boss too.

What I've found is most people want to leave the grind behind but see it as an unrealistic dream. If you broach the subject with passion and enthusiasm, you'll be surprised how willing people will be to support you. They can live vicariously through you.

Bosses also like to see themselves as a mentor and opportunity maker. As a boss, I always loved to help people get to the next level.

If you tell your boss up front that you want to gain experience and move on, you might be amazed at their response. In fact, I found this conversation won so consistently, it became a standard discussion in my first one-on-ones with new bosses. It told them that I was the one on the team who was "going places."

But what if your boss isn't supportive or has become too dependent on you? Easy: have the same conversation with their boss. Your boss's boss may have more ability to promote, move, or otherwise help you anyway.

4. Use educational benefits and ask for professional training.

While working in the call center, I learned that my employer would help pay for business school courses. I hopped right on this and took classes at night and online to earn my MBA.

I've used similar benefits to earn people-management, Six Sigma, Lean, Project Management Professional certifications, and more. I've also had employers send me to motivational speakers and seminars.

Even when the company doesn't officially offer educational benefits, all you might need to do is ask. I constantly made it known that I wanted to improve myself. After all, if your boss takes initiative to improve his or her team, they'll look good to their leadership.

If you are performing like a rock star, you'll get what you want.

5. Change jobs before you're ready–apply for internal jobs constantly.

At the first hint you're getting comfortable in your job, it's time to move. Otherwise you'll sink in and Cog to a halt.

Your goal here is to prepare yourself as fast as possible to be a true Grinder. If you're just sitting in the same role, you're not going to hit this goal. And you're not going to be meeting new people and expanding your network, either.

While I preferred promotions, I didn't worry about exclusively pursuing them. I always made it clear I preferred to move up, but I also regularly made lateral moves.

As I moved up and around within companies, my coworkers wondered why I was so favored. How did I get all of the jobs?

What they didn't realize was I was constantly talking to other managers, constantly applying for jobs, and constantly being burned left and right. While my coworkers were waiting for a golden platter, I was putting myself out there.

Did this tarnish how people viewed me or make it seem like I couldn't stick to something? Surprisingly, never. I think this was due to me being upfront with my managers.

6. Ask your way to success.

Chances are, if you're transitioning jobs and departments regularly, you're not going to be an expert at your job. This is exactly the idea. You're building experience and learning from the pros who have made careers out of their particular specialty. Use your ignorance to your advantage.

Seek out either the manager or top performer within an area and tag them as your mentor. People love to be perceived as an expert. This means someone will likely be happy to help you learn what you need—as long as you ask.

As you learn from them, apply what they teach you and ask increasingly complex questions. Don't just be a leech– demonstrate how they are making you a success.

7. Manage your network along the way.

As you go through all of this, stay in regular contact with the people who have helped you along the way. They helped you because they think highly of you. Don't forget this.

They may be your customer someday; after all, they're already convinced of your potential. My network has opened more doors for me after I left them behind than I ever imagined.

Keep in contact with people who have made a difference in your life. Help them without asking for anything in return.

Put a system in place, such as a calendar reminder, to check in with them monthly. Nurture your network. If you start to do this after you've left the grind behind, it's too late.

8. If you're feeling stuck, make a big play.

There will be times you don't see opportunities to continue your growth. But when it seems you cannot achieve your goals, it simply means it's time to get creative and find alternatives.

At times like this, it becomes particularly important to leverage your network. Talk with others in the company. Listen for pain points that may be outside of your sandbox and offer to solve them. Go make your own job. This is something I did regularly—I found a problem to solve, began solving it, and then got others, including my boss, on board. After all, would I rather work something assigned to me or something I found valuable and interesting?

If you don't think you have enough bandwidth to take on more work, remove that mental obstacle now. As a Grinder, you always want more work—you just need to figure out how to take it on. Delegate, partner, or eliminate. Some of the best results I ever achieved were from *not* working on something. More on this to come.

9. Remember you're reducing your risk.

Now that it's been years since I've left the grind behind, I can assure you that I'll never go back. It's unthinkable.

But, it was comforting to know that the companies I worked for saw my best. If I ever needed to return to Corporate America, I'd be welcomed. Further, since I gained such broad experience, I would be able to apply for a variety of jobs. My safety net is very large.

Following the principles in this chapter results in massively reducing the risk you might feel results from leaving the grind behind. Your worst case is going back to being a Cog. Since you're already a Cog, that's not that bad.

You're not going to lose your house if you use your parachute to safely return to a Cog job. I developed a huge network of people that still want me to be a Cog to this day and would happily welcome me back.

An Example of How I Maximized Now

At one of my companies, I heard a rumor that a key speaker for an upcoming conference had just quit...a mere two weeks before the event. He was slotted to speak to an international audience about a particularly controversial product our company produced.

While my peers gossiped about the situation, I shot off a note to our VP (at the time, she was three levels above me). I said I would go to the conference and take the speaker's role. Given the culture at my company, it was definitely a ballsy move.

While this VP had no idea who I was, I leveraged my network to talk to her and give me a good word. Before I knew it, I was at the conference in Canada in front of an audience that was ready to nail someone to the stake—it was indeed a controversial product. On stage, I was:

- Under-prepared.
- Unqualified.
- Ignorant.

Sounds like I was in the right place to fast track my way to the Grinder life.

While there, I quickly found out why my predecessor quit. The audience was livid about a variety of problems that had been growing over time. Fortunately, I was able to fall back on what

I learned from *How to Win Friends and Influence People*: I asked questions.

The session was highly interactive; the audience blew off steam; and I committed to follow up. As it turns out, this big move was effectively a job interview. The VP's right-hand man was in the audience observing my performance. When I returned from the trip, I was welcomed with yet another promotion.

To recap, I found a problem in the company. I made a big play by leveraging my network. I asked my way to success. I put myself way out of my comfort zone. I used basic human skills (from *How to Win Friends and Influence People*) to navigate a dicey situation successfully. My success had nothing to do with my product knowledge, my experience, or my job skills. But I sure learned and gained a lot.

Apart from this one example, these principles consistently played out well for me.

- I gained experience in operations, global people management, technical support, marketing, product management, product development, offer management, sales, project management, vendor management, and more. Won't that experience help as a Grinder?
- I had a reason—*a purpose*—to push through mundane and undesirable work. Knowing I was working for a bigger purpose made the work more tolerable. I can do annoying work if I know it is necessary for becoming a Grinder.
- I became highly valuable to my companies.

- I learned what I needed to ultimately pull the trigger and quit once the right opportunity came.
- Much to my surprise and pleasure, former co-workers asked to be my clients once I left the grind behind. One of my former companies still pays me to this day.

Conclusion

If you're not ready to be a Grinder, don't stagnate. Instead, prepare yourself to be ready for the opportunity once it presents itself. Make the most of your current situation. Build your experience; build your contacts, but most importantly, don't sit there and wait.

Take your corporate job for a joy ride—you won't be disappointed.

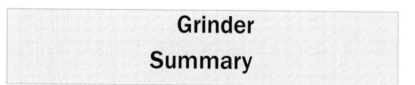

Grinder Summary

1. If you're not sure of your purpose for leaving the grind, don't sit idle. Use your time and current job to gain valuable experience and connections. Prepare for the opportunity once it presents itself.

2. In general, if you approach your job as a way to grow, learn, and experiment, you will end up benefiting your company and yourself. You will fast-track your way to becoming a Grinder.

3. Personally, I knew I was on course if I felt unprepared, in over my head, and to all external appearances, unfit and unqualified.

4. Get a job at a big company, even if it's a lower-level position.

5. Work hard at your job, even if it sucks or you feel it is below you

6. Tell your boss you want as much experience as possible so that you can quit. Tell your boss's boss too.

7. Use educational benefits and ask for professional training.

8. Change jobs before you're ready—apply for internal jobs constantly.

9. Ask your way to success.

10. Build your network of people along the way.

11. If you're feeling stuck, make a big play.

12. Keep in mind that you're reducing your risk by doing all of this.

Grinder Action: Start Your Engines

If you're working at a large company, take it upon yourself to look for open positions. This is easier if you tell your boss and your boss's boss that you want to move and grow. Focus on corporate or central-office jobs.

If you work at a smaller company or have some other factor limiting your movement, look for a job at another company. Get a job below your current position if necessary. If you're not ready to leave the grind behind, going with a lower-level job at a company with better growth potential will trump stagnation.

Grinder Habit:
Stay Uncomfortable

On a weekly basis, simply ask yourself the question "Am I uncomfortable with my job?" If so, you are growing and on track.

If you have a string of weeks filled with unchecked tasks or goals, you may be settling into your job and not developing. Corrective action is required.

By the way, this same principle holds true once you've left the grind behind. When running the show on your own, it is important to continue learning and pushing your results. Feeling uncomfortable and unqualified is something you'll learn to love.

CHAPTER 12

Free Up Time And Money

Even for those mentally prepared to leave the grind behind, there are a lot of practical hurdles. Some of the most common are having enough money or time or finding the right idea to take off with.

This chapter will help you eliminate time and money waste. It will then cover how to make the best use of your newfound free time.

Eliminating waste and focusing on what's important

I've met numerous folks who appear to have a great deal of success. But once I get to know them better, I discover they live a very unbalanced life. Their success comes at the expense of their family, health, and more. This is not what I want for myself or you.

Fortunately, I have a great background in Six Sigma, which is all about improving processes, reducing waste, and saving time at big companies. As it turns out, these principles apply terrifically to personal lives too.

Using my Six Sigma tools, I was able to reframe the connection between my time and my results. This allowed me to make changes and transition nicely from Cog to Grinder. And it allowed me to do so without sacrificing things that matter to me, like health and family.

Additionally, I know others who had equally demanding jobs and were also able to completely ramp up their own business on the side, providing a smooth transition out of the corporate world. It can be done.

Indeed, there is no shortage of ways to save time and money, but this first section contains the list of ideas that have made a big, practical difference for me personally. Hopefully they get your creative juices flowing.

Cogs have Waste; Grinders have Time

Finding time to launch a huge endeavor is never easy. In fact, if you have a spouse, kids, pets, and a full-time job, you may feel like you have zero minutes available for *you*. This is exactly how I felt.

But what's amazing is other people in your situation have accomplished massive success. So what's the difference? Why not you?

I was able to start up and leap into my own business directly from my demanding job. I have a young child, a dog, and a spouse. I had every excuse in the book.

But, I knew finding time was critical. It was a way for me to build a safety net. I didn't have to quit my day job first, which means I didn't expose myself to months of zero income while I got myself rolling. Rather, I was able to launch myself *and then* leave the grind behind.

As you know, our daily actions compound into big results. Time is no different. Time comes down to our day-to-day choices. If you are ruthless about your time, you will make time. And if you are going after a goal that is truly in-line with your passions, you will *want* to devote your time and energy to it.

As I started the process of leaving the grind behind, I was so excited to work on it. Finding time became easy. It was a game. Watch TV or work on my project? Not even a question! Once I got the ball rolling, the dominos began falling.

Think about time you waste in your life. If you stopped doing certain activities, would you care in a year? If you started doing other activities, would that matter in a year?

Through this section, I will give you specific examples of how I personally saved about $741 per month and 3 hours per day (that's 90 hours per month!) with a few simple changes. I used this time and money to help me leave the grind behind.

Freeing time frees your mind

I believe finding your breakthrough idea that will allow you to leave the grind behind is more about having everything else in your life lined up. Once you are mentally ready and have yourself surrounded by successful practices, the right opportunity will fall into your lap. You will be ready to take action on it.

This is not hocus-pocus; this is merely you being ready to say, *"Yes, I am going to take this problem by the horns...this is my opportunity."* On the other hand, if you're busy being busy, you simply let the opportunity go by or don't even notice it. You let someone else catch it.

Opportunities are passing us all by constantly, falling into the hands of others who are properly prepared to see and act on them.

Before I left the grind behind, I was worried about time. And I knew that if I was worried about an obstacle, I wouldn't be prepared to act on an opportunity. So I tackled this issue head on and made time a non-issue.

Free time—even a little per day—can give you what you need to focus on preparing to leave the grind behind by brainstorming plans, executing ideas, working with a Master-mind Group, being coached/mentored, or much more.

Money is a challenge if you want to leave the grind behind

As with time, money is a major mental block to quitting the daily grind. Providing for yourself is draining enough, but if you have a spouse, children, a house, and other obligations, stepping away from steady income feels massively scary.

I have all of these obligations plus am largely the sole provider for the family, so money is a massive consideration for me. And in talking to many other people wanting to become Grinders, money is a prime consideration for them too.

Building financial reserves will give you more confidence in your ability to quit your current job. And oftentimes, freeing up money and time go hand-in-hand.

Big and small ways to free up time and money

There are large ways you can create both time and money in your life. Large items are very important, but I wanted to make sure I knocked the simple stuff out too.

As a Grinder, you need to pull out all of the stops–and oftentimes the small items can add up and be equally as effective as difficult, larger moves. So, don't neglect reviewing your daily practices. Remember that your day-to-day actions compound and deliver massive effects.

This is precisely why Six Sigma and Lean projects deliver huge gains. They look at small, wasteful tasks that are repeated and cause compounded losses for companies.

So while $741 per month may sound like chump change to some of you, consider it's just part of a grander plan and resulted from eliminating some waste in my day-to-day practices. I'll take it.

Here we go. These are the quick and frugal ideas I put in place:

1. Switch from a debit card to a rewards credit card and automate payments

While basic in nature, the cumulative effect is outstanding. Paying bills and other recurring payments may only take a couple of hours per month, but that's enough freed time to get yourself set up with a monthly Mastermind Group or mentor—think about that.

Apart from the time benefit, you may be shocked at what you can get from rewards cards. I use a fantastic rewards card. I use it for not only recurring payments but also for day-to-day purchases. I avoid interest by paying it off completely in one payment at the end of each month.

The rewards are sufficient to cover one vacation per year. And now that I'm a Grinder, I have my business expenses running through the business version of the same card. The rewards can be combined, which means I can fund multiple trips.

As an additional idea, you can switch reward cards regularly. Card companies typically offer big incentives to sign up with them, which can boost how quickly you earn rewards.

Results:

- **Money freed**: over $1,500 per year, on the low end, thanks to rewards.
- **Time freed**: 2 hours per month.

2. Convince your boss to let you work from home

Working from home may seem like a pipe dream, but it's invaluable if you want to become a Grinder.

Personally, I was in a position where I never thought I'd be able to work from home. I managed a local team of people. All of my peers worked in the office. My boss was a big "in office" proponent. He showed up before everyone else and left after everyone too. As far as I knew, he slept there.

Despite this, I persisted in my mission to work from home and succeeded. Why? Because I knew the awesome power it held. I could deliver better results for the company and have massive freedom to pursue my best interests.

So how did I start? First, I negotiated with my management, constantly pressing to work from home. I started by pushing for one day per week as a pilot.

Since my job required a fair amount of face-to-face interaction and my boss was a blocker, I was unsuccessful. Was it time to give up? Heck no—Grinders are creative and find alternate ways to get what they want.

Instead of trying to work my current role into a work-from-home position, I began scouring the open positions within the company. I ultimately found a job that could be done entirely from home.

Incredibly, my mentor at the time was an influencer with the hiring manager. Some may say I was lucky; I'd say I was a Grinder. I was applying the principles in this book. Because of this, I was opening opportunities for myself and had the network to get it done.

My mentor helped me get the job, which was a promotion, paid much more, and gave me the ability to work from home full-time. Wow.

To me, working from home was that important–and it is doable, especially with today's technology. I'm convinced it can be done more than people think. I have personally done it in numerous jobs, from lower-level positions to senior management.

This of course won't work in every situation, but don't be afraid to be a pioneer at your company. You just need to prove you can work better from home. If you want more help, *The 4-Hour Work Week* is the classic read on why and how to work from home.

Even if you can only do this a couple of days per week, it's incredibly valuable, and not only from a money and time perspective. You'll also need to practice staying both on task and motivated without someone looking over your shoulder...two skills you'll need as a Grinder.

Monetary benefits:

- Auto costs, such as gas and maintenance.
- Food costs. You'll eat much cheaper and healthier at home.

Time benefits:

Lose the commute. This one can probably cut an hour out of most people's day.

- Getting ready in the morning and unwinding at night. When I started working from home, I could simply roll out of bed to my desk, and make myself "pretty" when time allowed. That's a heck of a lot easier than going through a standard-prep morning routine every day.
- Do you spend a lot of time on the phone at work? If you can go mobile while you're on calls, you can now go

about your chores while you're working. Simple things such as unloading the dishwasher and feeding the dog aren't much of a distraction and actually helped keep me engaged on long conference calls.

- Negative office chit-chat is cut. I love this one. Gossip is a killer in more ways than one. How much of your time is spent in non-productive, negative chit-chat at the office? You can still have witty banter on the phone, but non-productive time is significantly reduced and can be spent on better things.

Results:

- **Money freed**: using the IRS estimated mileage cost of 55 cents/mile, I freed up over $6,000 per year. I saved money on food but was pretty good about bringing my own lunch anyway. On food, I only saved $2, three days per week, netting another $312 per year. Total: $6,312 per year.
- **Time freed**: this netted about 32 hours freed per month. Wow—that's almost a work week freed up. I told you this one was powerful.

3. Pull the plug on expensive TV service—be a "Cord Cutter"

Cord cutting is trendy, so this is nothing new, but it helps you prepare to become a Grinder. Everyone watches a different amount of TV, but it can be a bigger time suck than most people realize.

Have you cut the cord yourself? Have you tracked how much time and money you actually put into TV? If you're serious about being a Grinder, this is a no brainer.

Also, many people pay over $100 per month for service. Switching to a cheaper (or no) service limits options and, ultimately, the desire to have the TV on, whether actively or just in the background.

Thinking about the time you spend watching TV, you probably want to replace it with not only just productive time, but also with more relaxing time. I recommend spending that time socially—the old-fashioned way. Unwind with your family or friends instead of the TV. Or if you've had enough of people during the day, meditate or exercise.

There are many articles on cord cutting, so I won't go into detail here. I don't watch TV much, but when I want to, I never feel limited. Cutting the cord has saved me a lot of money and a lot of time!

> "The bottom line is this: by focusing on happiness itself, you can lead a much better life than those who focus on convenience, luxury, and following the lead of the financially illiterate herd that is the TV-ad-absorbing Middle Class of the United States today (and most of the other rich countries)."
>
> ~ Mr. Money Mustache ~

Results:

- Money freed: about $1,080 per year
- Time freed: about 30 hours per month

4. Reduce and eliminate non-value-added work in your job

This, perhaps, has the biggest potential in this entire list. It means you should critically look at your job and figure out what you *don't* need to do.

If you're in a salaried position, any time you save goes directly back to you. Most salaried people I know work more than 40 hours; oftentimes quite a bit more. If you're becoming a Grinder, take back this time.

If you're in an hourly position, cutting time may not give you free hours. However, it can change what you're able to get from your job. If you cut waste, you can spend time on projects that will help you leave the grind behind. You can post improvements and enhance your performance, which will help you move into a better job. Or you can simply reduce your stress and avoid being "spent" at the end of every day.

Regardless of your job, most people do massive amounts of busy work—things they've been told to do but never really analyzed or critically thought about. Putting a Six Sigma or Lean lens on your work will allow you to cut waste.

Some ways you can do this are:

- Look at your role's objectives and your performance reviews. What is actually measured? Are you doing activities that are not directly influencing your results? Does anyone care about tasks you do?

- Look at the routine items you do, such as sending out reports. Do people really care about what you're sending? As you put together these reports, is there information that is hard to get that may be low value? Make sure to ask. During my waste-reduction projects, I would find employees spending hours building reports that were sent to leadership…who then promptly forwarded the reports to the trash. In big companies, people assume someone else cares, thus old processes never die.

- Think about the value chain from the customer's perspective. Does the customer care about what you're doing? Would they be willing to pay for it?

- Seek out someone who has Lean or Six Sigma training. I have experience in this area, so it's easy for me to find work to cut. If you don't see work you can optimize, find someone who can help you.

- Don't do other people's jobs. I had a really hard time with this and only finally let go during my last year as a Cog. Expect better performance from others and hold them accountable to their share of the work. Doing this freed up a huge amount of time and reduced stress for me.

- Talk to your boss about what you are doing and why you think you should eliminate certain work. Bosses generally like that you look at your job critically and try to improve it. They may be able to point out where you're over exerting. Get their input on what your value-add areas are and focus on those.

While paring down your work duties may not save you money, it can have huge mental and time benefits. You should also be able to post better results at work since you will be more focused on result-producing tasks only.

In fact, I found that when I did less at work, I actually was viewed better by management. I felt guilty at first, but quickly got over it. My results were better. While I did less, I was exceptionally focused on the few things that mattered.

No one cared that I didn't waste my time on busy work. My results were head-and-shoulders above my peers, who often worked twice as hard as me.

And by the way, the ability to determine and work on what matters is hugely important when you leave the grind behind. As a Grinder, you'll be overwhelmed and find yourself with a million things to do. If you don't do the right things, you won't succeed. Get in the habit of analyzing your work now.

Results:

- **Money freed**: Indirectly this behavior has earned me raises and bonuses, but it's tough to put a hard figure on it.
- **Time freed**: 20 hours per month.

My end results:

- **Total money freed:** over $8,800 per year, or $741 a month. As I was becoming a Grinder, this money covered the operating costs I was taking on and also provided some extra padding and comfort.
- **Total time freed:** about 84 hours per month—that's almost 3 hours every day! Couldn't you make serious progress toward leaving the grind behind with an extra 3 hours each day?

You never really know your behavior until you track it. People have off-base understandings of how their time is spent. In order to really nail this down, start by documenting how you spend your time for at least a couple of weeks.

This means you'll want to account for all 24 hours in a day. What sort of things should you track? Everything.

- Drove to work
- Watched TV
- Poked around on Facebook
- Put solid effort into value-add project at work
- Did non-value-add report at work
- Etc…

The more detailed and honest you are with yourself, the better. Once you have this list, you'll be able to go back and find time-freeing opportunities. You'll also be able to quantify the waste you've removed. Doing this exercise is how I was able tell you, with certainty, that I saved $741 per month and 3 hours per day.

Grinders Use Their Time Better

Once you apply the concepts in the prior section, you'll now want to optimize how you use your newfound time.

Let's start by asking some questions. When you think back on your life, what do you remember? What moments create the movie of your life? Do you remember surfing Facebook? Watching TV? Checking email? Probably not.

You more likely remember outstanding personal interactions, emotional situations, and things you created.

Thought of in this way, you create the life you live and remember by the day-to-day time decisions you make. I like to sum this up in a statement, *"highest and best use of every moment."*

I have this saying written down on a card next to my affirmations and love to review it regularly. It helps me make the best moment-by-moment decisions about my time.

And it's amazing what moment-by-moment decisions can do. No matter who we are, we all share the same time limitations. So why do only some people lead such incredibly full, rich, healthy, and productive lives? Simple: they know how to make the highest-and-best use of their time. They use time to their advantage.

I'll give you two tips to turn on the switch for leading just such a life. And when you make the best use of your time, your remembered time—and therefore life—truly expands.

Additionally, using these tips, I've come to realize I can get much more work done than most people, yet end up working fewer hours. In fact, right now, I have a wide variety of roles, many of which most people would consider full-time jobs. Yet I pull it off and maintain a balanced life.

Tip 1. Segment your time and use Pomodoro

Using your time productively does not always mean working. Perhaps having a picnic with the family will allow you to recharge and bond with your family. Whatever the use of your time though, being present allows you to realize the most from that time. By segmenting your time, you are more likely to make the best of it.

Indeed, when Warren Buffet and Bill Gates were asked what the single most important factor for success was, they both independently answered "Focus." The ability to sit down and work deeply on one item at a time.

The good news is this is a very simple practice to incorporate into your life. You can start by segmenting your time at a high level. Some common time segments include:

- Family
- Work
- Leisure
- Social
- Spiritual
- Learning

Try setting aside time for each of these throughout your days and weeks. Once you have these times set up, you can sub-segment that time, working on one individual work item at a time, for example.

Put yourself into each of them 100% during their given timeslot. I call this *deep time.*

By focusing your time, you'll feel as though you create time out of nowhere. Numerous studies have shown the tremendous "switching cost" you pay as your brain switches from task to task, concept to concept, or segment to segment.

In fact, switching between activities rather than focusing on one at a time results in a 40% productivity loss, according to the American Psychological Association (*Who Multi-Tasks and Why? Multi-Tasking Ability, Perceived Multi-Tasking Ability, Impulsivity, and Sensation Seeking* by Sanbonmatsu DM, Strayer DL, Medeiros-Ward N, Watson JM).

Multi-tasking doesn't work, but you're likely unaware of exactly how much it impacts your productivity until you deliberately segment and manage your time.

The problem is, I don't like to over-plan my day. Perhaps blocking off time and strictly adhering to your plan works for you. But I find I can't stick to something this structured. Daily distractions and interruptions can blow my plans up quickly. Fortunately, I've found a great alternative.

The technique I prefer is called *The Pomodoro Technique.* You spend 25 minutes focused on one task. Once the 25 minutes is up, you take a 5-minute break to do whatever you want. Then you do another 25-minute chunk of productive work on a specific task. You take a lot of breaks, but you will find yourself highly focused during those 25 minute intervals of deep work. For example, I may work email for 25 minutes. After a break, my next block is spent on writing an article. The trick is to truly focus on one item at a time.

If you're interested in The Pomodoro Technique, simply search for it and you'll find apps for your computer or other devices that will manage the timing for you. It's a very simple way to practice segmenting your time and focusing.

2. Use a handwritten "things to do today" list

This technique is no secret, but don't let its simplicity fool you. Nothing will make you use your time better than writing—*by hand*—a list of things you need to do for the day.

Each day, I start with a big blank sheet of paper with 16 lines. Before logging in to my computer, I write down what I want to accomplish that day. The goal is to know that if I complete the list, I will have felt productive for the day. I will have kicked the ball forward enough to drive the sort of momentum I need as a Grinder.

> **"The very act of working from a list will increase your productivity by 25-50 percent the very first day."**
>
> **~ Brian Tracy, Get Smart! ~**

Getting into a list-making routine is particularly great when you feel stressed, overwhelmed, or disorganized. If you're anxious or have trouble sleeping, keep a notepad handy and simply jot down ideas to tackle later. Then, relax. In the morning, you can review your notes and add items to your to-do list.

There is a real mental advantage to taking a clear, focused moment to write out your day's to-do list by hand. By physically writing the list, your mind engages on multiple levels. For more on this, check out the book *Write it Down, Make it Happen* by Anne Klauser, PhD. Or, if you don't care about the background and supporting information, *It Works* is a lightning fast read and costs just a few bucks.

What's most shocking about making a handwritten list is that I usually finish the tasks on my list much faster than I expect, and I certainly accomplish more than if I hadn't written a list. Think about that. *I do more in less time.*

Often, I'm done by lunch. In other words, I write out a big, daunting list in the morning. I know if I accomplish those items, I'll feel great about my productivity. I expect the list to take me a full day. Instead, I finish with half my day left. Awesome.

Having accomplished my list, I can move on to other activities and time segments. I can move on to creative, big-picture items—precisely because my brain isn't cluttered with outstanding things to do. Once you begin to see this in action, you'll realize how much time you waste if you are unfocused. It's absolutely incredible.

And by the way, I am not an organized person by nature. Planning like this is actually difficult for me. If you've failed at more complex planning systems before, try the simple daily, handwritten list. The simplicity works wonders for me and ensures I get *it* done.

Grinder
Summary

1. Finding your breakthrough idea that will allow you to leave the grind behind is about having everything else in your life lined up.

2. Once you are mentally ready and are surrounded by successful practices, the right opportunity will fall into your lap. To get to this spot, you need extra time.

3. Time is a challenge for everyone…but can be managed.

4. To free up time and money, don't overcomplicate. Look at your day-to-day practices. Small changes compound and deliver massive effects.

5. Working from home is one of the best moves you can make during your transition from Cog to Grinder. Make it happen.

6. Be ruthless with your time. It's your most valuable asset.

7. Segment your time and focus. Look into The Pomodoro Technique to get started.

8. Write a "Things To Do Today" list.

9. Read *The 4-Hour Workweek* by Tim Ferriss for more tips on removing waste and getting the most from your time.

Grinder Action:
What Steals Your Time and Money?

Alright, you've seen how waste can add up to lost time and money. Be honest with yourself and identify at least 20 ways in which you are wasting time and money.

Leverage your Mastermind Group, your banker, a lender, your insurance agent, etc. We all waste money and need a good financial health check-in on a regular basis. Maybe you can lock in lower interest rates, drop mortgage insurance, or renegotiate monthly bills.

Grinder Habit:
Document How You Spend Time

This one is easy. Before you read email or do other "inbound" work, make the list of things you want to do for the day. Define your time before others do. Use the Grind Today sheet at **grindbehindbook.com/tools**.

Also, get in the habit of using The Pomodoro Technique. In particular, use it during work hours. Focus on one task for 25 minutes then take a 5-minute break.

CHAPTER 13

How to Take Grinder-Worthy Action

By this point, you should be ready to do something big—like leaving the grind behind. But what's your first step? Big goals are daunting. And if they were easy to achieve, everyone would.

I use a consistently winning strategy for tackling big goals. This chapter will allow you to take a massive goal and make it something tactical. Something you can start doing now. And success wants you to get started now.

You'll achieve big goals by:

1.   Working goals backward from the end-state to actionable steps you can take today.
2.   Using basic math to identify the easiest variables to focus on.

Achieve Big Goals by Working them Backward

A while back, I was having a hard time with one of my main goals. This particular goal involved earnings.

The goal simply did *not* seem achievable. Even after applying many of the techniques I discuss in this book, I was having a hard time seeing how it would happen. So the question became: do I adjust the goal down or do I figure out how to press forward?

Big goals are tough

My goal and affirmative statement was pretty straight-forward: "I am incredibly proud to have made $xxx,xxx or more by 8/22/2014. I love that it affords the choices, freedom, and ability to support the dreams of those around me."

The dollar value was more than double my six figure Cog earnings. This is a big goal, but I wanted it to be challenging so I would be forced to take breakthrough actions.

The key steps I had already taken toward this goal were: 1) I quit my job, and 2) I relocated to be close to a mentor. These were extreme steps but definitely the sort of steps required to get a 100%+ raise in one year.

I was thinking about my goal constantly and writing it down daily. I was visualizing the goal, but it still felt very out of focus.

I had similar stretch-goals in other parts of my life that I set at about the same time. Several months in, achieving those goals seemed clear and possible. Some were even knocked out already. The "how" of achieving them had come to me in one form or another, but this one continued to elude.

Revise the goal or press forward?

I was very close to revising it down, but instead, I decided to continue to trust the system and push on. I continued writing it down every night. I continued running through the techniques mentioned in this book. I continued to obsess about it. I told myself that if it's not a stretch goal, I wouldn't find a creative way to get to where I want. I shouldn't settle.

The breakthrough

Any time you apply this much thought toward something, you will ultimately have a breakthrough. In this case, it took about three months, which is much longer than I generally expect.

My breakthrough came from my Mastermind Group, though I'm a bit embarrassed I didn't come up with this on my own. The technique was not new to me at all. In fact, it's something I've advised many people to do in many other situations. This shows the power of Mastermind Groups and why you need a body of trusted people working on your life!

The solution was to work it backward. This technique involves starting with the end in mind and working things backward until they become measurable, actionable chunks—a work breakdown structure.

Instead of telling someone to make a skyscraper, you tell them to hit that nail with a hammer. If you get enough people doing the right, simple tasks, you get a skyscraper.

> "You don't set out to build a wall. You don't say 'I'm going to build the biggest, baddest, greatest wall that's ever been built.' You don't start there. You say, 'I'm going to lay this brick as perfectly as a brick can be laid.' You do that every single day. And soon you have a wall."
>
> ~ Will Smith ~

The advice, specifically, was to stop thinking in the sky and instead be more concrete and tactical. In order to do this, I needed to break down my goal and work it backward. The goal is to isolate the easiest variable to manipulate.

> "Any goal can be achieved if you break it down into enough small parts."
>
> ~ Henry Ford ~

Work breakdown structure applied to personal goals

Do you apply project management to your personal life? It's something I constantly utilized in my professional life to work stretch goals from executives that caused everyone else to run for the hills. The work/breakdown structure and "plan backward" technique caused teams to go from "freaking out" to, "hey, this looks possible," to "hey, we achieved it!"

It's all about starting with the end in mind and brainstorming backward to where you are now. You identify the actionable chunks that come up along the way.

"Actionable" is the key word. You need to settle on tasks that are small enough that they can be easily conceptualized and completed. You want to transition from some high-in-the-clouds goal to a step you can take right now.

It seems simple yet can provide unexpected results, making the path more achievable. This technique works because you focus on what you actually need along the way.

If you plan forward instead, you end up thinking about all of the little things that *could* happen and stop before you even get started. In the professional world, this manifests as endless, frustrating brainstorming sessions.

My goal...worked backward

To work my goal backward, I began with a mind map of it. I wrote down my goal in the middle, and then started breaking it down and going through the following steps:

1. Goal: to make $xxx,xxx by 8/22/2014
2. Break that down into my four main income streams:
   a. Stream 1: management (marketing, finance, strategy) consulting, which is a contracted, fixed amount for the year.
   b. Stream 2: other consulting which is variable yet consistent, so I can estimate it fairly well.
   c. Stream 3: house sales (using my real estate license) which are highly variable.
   d. Stream 4: a business performance bonus that is dependent on Streams 1 and 3.
   e. Stream 5: investment income.
3. To achieve my goal, I assigned dollar values to each stream. What would they need to be to hit my goal? I've worked it backward.
4. Stream 3 was my key-focus area. Why? It had an easy-to-assign variable and impacted another stream.
5. I drilled down on Stream 3 and changed it to something measurable in terms other than dollars. In this case I chose number of houses sold.
6. To get to a quantity of houses, I needed to do some math. I multiplied average sales price by the average commission, then pulled out the portion of the commission I kept ($178,000 * 3% * 50%). Simple math...simple technique.
7. In order to hit the dollar value I assigned for Stream 3 in the subsequent nine months, I needed to sell 54 houses. This translates to six per month. Now we're talking! Six

sales per month sounds easy, achievable, and something I can grind on every day. It sounds way simpler than the dollar goal I started with.

8. Compare this to the market. Is this level achievable? As it turns out, 6 sales per month is high but not outrageous. Other people near me do more. It's less than a percent of the local market. When I compare my broken-down goal to what others are doing, it becomes pretty clear my goal is not crazy.

9. While others in my market may be doing 6 sales per month, they will not achieve my earnings level. That's because I have set up a fairly robust structure that expands based on this one variable. I have scalability and multipliers built into my plan. Performance in Stream 3 boosts Streams 1 and 4 as well. Bingo.

Working it backward to actionable steps

I just took a very large goal, worked it backward, and came up with a simple thing for me to focus on: sell 6 houses per month. That's it. That is way easier than focusing on an elusive, large-earnings number. I can visualize this.

I also discovered a few other things along the way. Here's what I'm going to do as a result of applying this technique:

- Continue to learn about, apply myself to, and work hard on Stream 1.
- Request a different compensation structure from my bigger consulting clients in Stream 2, moving from hourly consulting to results-based percentages.
- Let Stream 4 take care of itself as a result of Streams 1 and 3.
- Focus my attention on Stream 3—6 sales per month!

The "6 sales" action became my key variable. If I took care of it, the rest should fall into place. It's the most important variable in hitting my goal and therefore should see a corresponding amount of my focus and attention.

In fact, I took this math much further to figure out how toachieve 6 sales per month. I used industry benchmarks and a professional coaching system to determine how many leads I'd need to get 6 sales. I determined how many phone calls I'd need to make to generate that many leads. I then had a simple bogey of making a certain number of phone calls per day. That's even simpler.

Massive goal broken down to simple execution. Using my earlier analogy, I successfully took the goal of "building a skyscraper" and simplified it to the nails that needed to be hammered.

Did it all go to plan?

As it turned out, working "6 sales" per month was a lot of work. It was time consuming and didn't really lend itself to my bigger-picture purpose or goals.

But I didn't let that sway me. Instead, I applied the concepts you'll see in the next chapter and had someone else sell for me. I partnered with them and put a team of real estate agents in place under us.

Together, they sold the equivalent of more than just 6 sales and the system no longer relied on my time. It was scalable. I found a better way to hit my 6 number. This had Grinder written all over it.

Better yet, now that I had my head clear about what I was focusing on, my creativity began to flourish, and I began introducing other significant income streams. I did in fact hit my goal, with much less work than I was expecting.

The moral of the story is simple: take the time to transform big goals into actionable steps. Do the math. Isolate the variable that affects whether you'll achieve your goal. As you focus on this variable, hopefully you will find simpler and simpler ways of making it happen.

Grinder Summary

1. Big goals aren't harder than small goals as long as you break them down into tactical chunks.
2. Apply the techniques from Section 1 to get into the Grinder mindset and obsess about your goals until you're able to convert them into actionable items.

3. Use a work breakdown structure and mind maps to work goals backward and break steps into small actionable tasks.

4. Isolate the one variable that will have the biggest impact on your goal. Focus your energy and attention on it.

5. Use math where possible to figure out how often you need to do a particular task to achieve the goal you want. Ideally you'll find you need to do a task X times per day; then you simply need to execute.

Grinder Action: Break Down Your GRINDER 3 Goals

Go back to your goals and pick your big three. You're welcome to break your goals down as you see fit, but I recommend using a work breakdown structure and mind maps, to force you to start chunking big ideas into small, actionable items.

As you break down your goals, you need to make your tasks small and relatable. Typically this means these are tasks you can accomplish in a couple of days or less.

Once you have your big goal broken down into tangible steps, either create a checklist or print off a map of the tasks. As you complete the tasks, cross them off. This gives you a visual way to show you're taking steps toward your goal each and every day. It's how you go from a daunting, where-do-I-start idea to taking your first step.

Grinder Habit: Take Action on Your GRINDER 3 Every Single Day

Alright, this one is simple. Don't wait. Success loves action and speed. Get it done. Take at least one action per day on each of your GRINDER 3.

For now, this means mapping out and breaking down your goals. Once that is done, find at least one thing to check off every single day. Keep some easy to help your momentum. I'm not saying you need to spend 10 hours per task…maybe one takes 5 minutes. The effort doesn't really matter. What matters is constantly moving forward. If you do this, can you imagine where you'll be one year from now? How about three?

Personally, I hope this is laughable, and you do much more than one action per day. But when you start, commit to at least one per day for each big goal.

Pick up the phone and ask for that introduction. Close Facebook and spend one hour researching your market. No one is going to do it for you or ask you to do it. You're in charge. Kick the ball forward starting today.

CHAPTER 14

Skills Grinders Learn

As you build additional income streams and start transitioning to a full-time Grinder, you'll find certain skills are valuable regardless of your endeavor. These skills put your value in the hands of many.

Coming up with excellent, entrepreneur-worthy ideas is not all that unique. People come up with "that idea" all the time. Perhaps they are a brilliant software engineer capable of developing a valuable piece of software. Or an exceptionally talented writer who has amazing stories to share.

Why don't these people become Grinders? They do not know how to let the world know what they've done.

So instead of selling it themselves, they hand their work over to their employer. Who wins? In the case of the engineer, the employer gets a game-changing bit of software to sell and profit from heavily. The engineer gets a pat on the back and perhaps even a record raise (maybe 15%). Is this a windfall? Absolutely not. But this exact situation occurs daily.

Don't be a Cog who's building someone else's legacy. Instead, develop the three skills that will help you get the middleman—your employer—out of the picture.

Here's some good news: most people lack these three skills. Because of this, it's easier for you to stand out and win than you think.

The other good news is all of these skills are learnable—quickly learnable.

Money machines

When you pull these skills together, you will have what it takes to create a money machine

A money machine is something you can put $1 into and receive $2 from. Ideally you create something once (think a piece of software or an educational course), then sit back and watch it generate more dollars in sales than it costs to market.

Money machines are what Grinders strive to create.

Grinders Skill 1: Execution

Execution is the skill of *completing* something. It's as simple as that. However, many of us never really complete the things we start. We've all had great ideas that we became jazzed about, started, then let stagnate.

A Grinder knows ideas have zero value until they are executed. Does this statement sound familiar? "Oh, I had that idea years ago! That should be *me* making millions."

> "To me, ideas are worth nothing unless executed. They are just a multiplier. Execution is worth millions."
>
> ~ Steve Jobs ~

So how do you execute as a Grinder? Simple—you get stuff done. Seriously, you pick your idea and you focus on it every single day until it's complete.

Throughout this book, you've seen a ton of ideas about breaking down a big idea and beginning to work on it. There's nothing magic here: you just need to get down to business.

> "Your life will not change when you know what to do. Your life will change when you do what you know."
>
> ~ Jaykaran Sagar ~

Once you've realized your idea, the execution doesn't stop. Grinders tweak, perfect, and push, push, push until the optimal outcome is achieved.

Grinding for yourself: what a change

This new sort of grinding is highly empowering. As a Grinder, you're grinding *for yourself*. The fruits of your grind no longer go to someone else.

You build your own brand. You're no longer a Cog. Grinding is now exhilarating. As long as you grind harder than the next guy, you will win.

Execution is really just about deliberately moving forward every day. To recap some of the key ideas:

1. Write out your to-dos every single morning and complete them. Ensure these to-dos include actions toward realizing your idea. The simplest approach is to use the "Grind List" to-do sheet provided at **grindbehindbook.com/tools.**

2. Be ruthless with your time. When you work, work on what's important, not what keeps you busy. Ask yourself if the tasks you're working on will matter in one year.

3. Habits compound, so get in the habit of dedicated daily action.

4. If you expose your idea to the world and don't achieve the results you want, don't give up. Grind, grind, and grind. Keep pushing until you get the results you want.

5. To get motivated to grind harder than the next guy, read *The 10X Rule* by Grant Cardone.

6. Next, read *Deep Work* by Cal Newport for ideas on increasing execution via deliberate focus and segmented time.

Grinders Skill 2: Sales

Sales skills are under-appreciated until you need them. In fact, many Cogs will turn their noses up at sales and associate it with sleazy used-car types. This is a major mistake—one I made for far too long.

Sales is not sleazy, though sleazy people can be in sales. It simply involves sharing the value you bring with other people. Thought of in this light, it is really a service.

Let's say you have something that will benefit people so much that they will gladly give you money for it. If this is the case, you are doing people a disservice by not telling them about it. *Not selling is sleazy.*

There are many ins and outs to sales, most of which have to do with fundamental human psychology. But to sum it up, sales comes down to being able to understand your audience and convey your value from their point of view. Grinders don't go door-to- door or make cold calls. Instead, we know how to share ideas and let people know about our value.

Developing this skill is a Grinder requisite. But the good news is, you have plenty of opportunity to sell during your transition.

Prior to leaving the grind behind, you'll need to convince people to join your Mastermind Group. You'll need to convince someone to be your mentor. You'll need to convince your company to give you more responsibility and move you around regularly. You need to convince them to let you work from home. You have a lot of convincing to do. Convincing=sales.

When it comes to your first few side gigs (such as consulting), your ability to convince and sell yourself will really be tested. You'll have limited experience and few success stories to lean on. You need to believe in yourself so much that others do too.

Once you can sell, your personal stock will grow exponentially. If you have the skills to execute *and* grow companies, you will be hired pretty much anywhere. This is what businesses really want. They want growth.

Developing your sales skills is necessary in order to be a Grinder, but it also adds another layer to your safety net as you leave the grind behind. Worst case, your life as a Grinder is a fat failure and you have to go back to Cog life. But since you've developed these valuable skills, you'll get a better Cog job upon your return.

But I'm here to make you a successful Grinder, not just a great Cog. And as a Grinder, you're going to need to sell yourself every day. Do you want someone to work for your company? Do you want to hire a PR firm? Do you want the bank to give you a loan? Do you want venture capital? You will be selling during each one of these conversations. Grinders must embrace being a salesperson.

I am far from being a sales master. But I have learned a lot during my Grinder years . Here are my tips to get you started on your sales journey:

1. Instead of "selling to someone," simply learn to share the true value of what you offer. Don't embellish or exaggerate. Be frank about what your value is and what it is not.
2. Put yourself in the shoes of your customers. You are not selling to yourself, so make sure you are framing from their perspective. What are their needs? Let them know how they benefit.

3. If you're not sure how to do #2, it's because you are talking instead of listening. When I am "selling," I am listening. 80%+ of my time involves asking questions and getting to know more about my target audience. This allows me to understand how my value applies to them. Good salespeople listen. Think about selling yourself for a promotion—instead of saying all the great things you have done, ask questions about what needs to be done. What is the company looking for in whoever takes this new position? Now you can speak intelligently about why you may or may not be the right one for that Cog promotion.

4. Put your customers' interests first. Do the right thing by them, and sales follow. I never push people or go for the easy sale. I am objective and help people understand the pros and cons so they can make a good decision for themselves. This develops a loyal following and customers who refer business to me…that's equal to a free marketing and sales staff, which is far more valuable than an individual quick sale.

5. Be genuinely enthusiastic. Know your value inside and out and be proud of it. If you're not proud of it, go back to execution until you have something you are over-the-top enthusiastic about. It doesn't feel like selling when you love what you have to share.

6. To improve even more, read How to Win Friends and Influence People by Dale Carnegie and Secrets of Closing the Sale by Zig Ziglar.

Grinder Skill 3: Marketing

Sales and marketing are very closely related, but I consider marketing slightly less personal and much more data driven.

You do, however, need a solid foundation in sales to churn out good marketing. If you don't know how to sell to one person, how can you sell to thousands?

Marketing is about being able to apply sales systematically with tools and automation to a mass audience. It's about being able to stand out from the crowd and progress people from not knowing you to buying from you. It's about being able to sell from behind a keyboard.

While the audience is broader, the goal is the same. Marketing is a *sales* channel and should be expected to *sell*. Every dollar spent in marketing should be tied to sales. If I put $1 in, I want $2 out.

People mistakenly believe marketing is about "getting your name out there" or "building a brand." Marketing should be much more. It should fully result in concrete sales results.

I am very particular about marketing. It was my area of emphasis during my MBA and is my favorite aspect of being a Grinder. As such, I can quickly spot people who understand marketing and people who don't.

If I ask someone how to market a given product or service and they reply with a solution, I know they're an amateur. If they instead reply with a construct for a test, I know they're savvy. Testing is what marketing is all about.

We can never exactly know the best way to reach our audiences. We never know the best way to get them to realize our value enough to start handing over their money. So good marketers try different ideas, measure results, and constantly improve.

Because good marketing is about testing, marketers must have goals for their work and know how to systematically track those goals. A good marketer will be able to test the impact of images, taglines, words, length, customer flow, messaging sequencing, and much more.

I could write an entire book on this topic, but let me give you a few starter tips:

1. Don't expect people to land on your website and buy. Most people will start off cold and need to be warmed up to your value proposition. This is the job of marketing—*nurturing*.

2. To market effectively, you need to learn about setting marketing goals, collecting data, and running tests.

3. Everything you do online will have marketing implications because it will impact the sales process. Therefore, you should look to build well-rounded marketing skills. These include copy writing, sales funneling, and nurturing.

4. Don't assume you have to spend a huge amount up front to market your new idea. Advertising platforms such as Google and Facebook allow your advertising to be hyper targeted. You can measure results against goals and scale up quickly. You should hold your advertising accountable and expect a return.

5. Good marketing data will give you the coveted *money machine*. If you know you can put $1 into marketing and

receive $2 as a result, congratulations. You are a bona-fide Grinder. Your job now becomes determining how much money you can put in before results level off. And once you hit a leveling-off point, don't stop! Keep your execution hat on and test, test, test. Keep pushing. Keep tweaking. Keep grinding.

6. If you have a great idea, but are stumbling with marketing, it is best to partner with a person or company that has expertise marketing within your niche. Even though I have strong marketing knowledge marketing, I continue to pay for consultants and seek out new mentors. Marketing makes or breaks companies, so I invest highly in it. I just make sure I learn from the engagement. I don't want to completely hand responsibility over. I want to develop my skills.

7. To understand what I mean by testing, read *Scientific Advertising* by Claude Hopkins. It was written in the 1920s, but its principles have transcended time. It will make you thankful we live in an age that has tools such as Google Analytics.

8. Read *Cashvertising* by Drew Eric Whitman to get insight into how human psychology works in relation to marketing.

9. Also read *The Copywriter's Handbook* by Robert W. Bly to learn how to choose words wisely.

Refine on Someone Else's Dime

What if you don't have these three skills today? Should you leave the grind behind? Not yet, cowboy. Great ideas fail all the time because people cannot execute them, sell them, or market them.

You must have at least working marketing knowledge and the ability to augment with the right people. But you will succeed much faster if you build these skills yourself.

So don't learn the fundamentals while your own Grinder idea is on the line. Build a safety net and gain real-life experience before you quit.

But how should you go about building these skills while you're stuck at a Cog job? There are two good approaches.

1. Change jobs

The first approach goes back to getting the most from your Cog job. To build these three skills, simply change jobs. This is exactly what I did. I took jobs in marketing and sales. I also took jobs in offer management, which involved taking a product and building out the entire process to launch and sell the product—essentially idea execution.

2. Study and consult

A second approach may be required if you're unable to move into these types of jobs while you're a Cog. What you can do instead is spend your free time learning everything you can about these topics. Then, use your knowledge to pick up a consultative side gig.

Look for someone within your network or work with your Mastermind Group to find someone you can help.

Chances are you can find someone out there who is trying to leave the grind behind but didn't read this chapter. Now they're floundering and their dreams of greatness are collapsing. You can help.

Even if you're not an expert with years of results behind you, you can quickly learn more than most people will ever know. If you read the books I recommended in this chapter, you will have a master's course of information at your fingertips. Time to start trying out your ideas.

Don't be ashamed and don't feel like you won't add value. If you know someone who could use help with marketing, tell them the truth. Tell them what you know and what you're up to. Tell them you both stand to benefit. And tell them you'll only get paid for results.

Here's the thing: people who have depth of expertise in execution, sales, and marketing know they are hot. So, they charge massive amounts of money. Isn't it exceptionally valuable to be able to take an idea and turn it into money? Yes. Because of this, hiring this out becomes too expensive for most small business owners. So step in, help, learn, refine, get real-world expertise, and earn your worth.

After gaining corporate experience in these skills, I also took this second approach. I found someone selling an informational product through a decent website. It was a great product: I genuinely believed in it. The problem is, the site was weak and sales were just "okay." It wasn't enough to make him a real Grinder.

I took a look at what was going on, and realized I knew much more than he did in certain areas. Of course, he knew much more than me in other areas. We had a complimentary skillset.

While my knowledge wasn't perfect, it was a major step up and was enough to get some strong improvement rolling. We decided to partner up. I'd make money on a sliding scale.

The worst case was that I'd learn what didn't work. The best case was I'd learn what works, what doesn't, get to participate in a scalable business, and ultimately become a real expert—all without risking a failed business of my own.

This particular deal ended up working out terrifically for both me and the business owner. Within about one year, sales were up over 700%. I'm earning scalable income from it still. The experience has allowed me to land similar gigs too. With all of this, I'm in a much better position to launch my own products...I learned and refined on someone else's dime.

Grinder Summary

1. Grinders will fail unless they learn execution, sales, and marketing.
2. Since most people don't excel at these skills, it's easier for you to stand out and win.
3. Ideas have no value. Execution of ideas does.
4. Execution is about daily choices and compounding progress.

5. The biggest trick to sales is to put yourself in your customers' shoes. You have to listen first.

6. Marketing is about selling broadly to a scalable audience.

7. The answer is to test. Which headline works better? Which picture? Test. Data, data, data.

8. Good marketing practices will give you a money machine. Put $1 in, get $2 back.

9. Refine your skills on someone else's dime. Don't take off your training wheels for your own project. Earn money by testing and improving your skills on someone else's.

10. One approach is to gain experience within a Cog job. Seek a promotion, lateral move, or transfer into a role of execution, sales, or marketing.

11. Another approach is to become a consultant for someone who needs help with execution, sales, and marketing. Study up first, then seek a job with pay-based results.

Grinder Action: Get Reading

I provided some outstanding reading recommendations in this chapter. In fact, I would call it a master's course for turning ideas into money.If you drive to your Cog job, get audio versions and get learning. Here's that list again:

- Execution
    - *The 10X Rule* by Grant Cardone
    - *Deep Work* by Cal Newport

- Sales
  - How to Win Friends and Influence People by Dale Carnegie
  - Secrets of Closing the Sale by Zig Ziglar
- Marketing
  - Scientific Advertising by Claude Hopkins
  - *Cashvertising* by Drew Eric Whitman
  - The Copywriter's Handbook by Robert W. Bly

In addition to starting your master's course, get practical experience. Seek a job at your company in which you'll gain exposure to and grow these skills. Also consult your Mastermind Group to see if they know someone who could use help in these areas.

CHAPTER 15

How Grinders
Think About Money

> "An Ivy League Education costs about $252,000 and will teach you exactly how to make a $60,000 per year salary."
>
> ~Bloomberg, 2015~

I spent a good amount of money on my education. And out of school I landed a "sweet" customer service call center job...not exactly what I was hoping for. In fact, it was Cog Hell.

While it wasn't where I wanted to be, many people end up in a much worse situation—leaving college saddled with significant education debt, which drastically offsets future income.

Don't get me wrong—there is value in standard education. Personally, I gained great contacts and developed skills I was able to use to differentiate myself from my peers early on.

But when it comes to learning how to really make money, don't expect traditional education to be your solution. In fact, I can say throughout my entire education, the process of making money was never really explored.

Traditional education teaches you to be a Cog. Grinder education teaches you that making real money is a game. It's a fun game. In fact, if you can be passionate about the game of money, opportunities open everywhere for you.

Mediocre money conditioning

I just said school doesn't teach you how to make money, but I'm going to take it a step further….it actually conditions us all wrong. We are conditioned to be Cogs. We are conditioned to realize mediocre financial results.

We are explicitly conditioned against being a Grinder. It takes too much money. I'll need startup capital and big loans. I'll have months where I lose money. It's just too risky. I could lose everything.

With beliefs and statements like this, how does anyone become a successful Grinder?

It's time for a change. It's time to start thinking about how real money is made and held. It's time to enable yourself through reconditioning.

So how does a Grinder think? Grinders think about two key metrics: net worth and scalability. Net worth gives us our big picture, long-term view. Scalability gives us strategic direction in our day-to-day actions.

The Big Picture is Net Worth

Thinking about net worth first, rather than specific account balances, monthly income, and monthly expenses is something that you'll need to do as a Grinder.

Why? It directs you to focus on long-term goals and removes the day-to-day noise. It also forces your mind to think about the big moves you can make that will impact your net worth.

While still in my corporate job, I got in the habit of looking at my net worth and using it to set my financial goals, whether monthly, yearly, or longer. I pinned graph paper on my wall right in front of my face and plotted my net worth.

This was a great visual cue, tapping right into the mental tactics from Section 1. And it was a *blast* to watch it begin to change and jump as I moved forward.

No longer did I want to make a certain salary; I wanted to see my net worth increase by a specific amount. This change in mindset is simple yet deceptively powerful. I wasn't thinking like a Cog. I wasn't thinking about standard money drivers. I was instead thinking about big-picture items that could cause massive changes in my overall worth.

In my old way of thinking, I focused on raises and bonuses. I knew an average annual salary increase at my company was 0-3%. Top performers might get a 7-10% increase and maybe a bonus. I used to get excited for these increases. However, viewed through the lens of net worth, I figured out exactly how insignificant they really were.

If I worked my Cog-butt off and brought in raises like this consistently, sure, those raises would increase nicely over time. But unless I was receiving promotions too, I'd eventually start hitting range limits. If I was promoted, I'd lose balance in my life and stray from my broader goals.

In other words, if I was looking at the right-hand gauge on the dashboard, it was clear that annual salary increases wouldn't move the needle. This was pretty eye opening and put my enthusiasm for raises in check.

The reality is, in order to move the net-worth needle, you need to make big plays. Big plays require big goals and big actions. But as we've already determined, bigger isn't necessarily more difficult. It's just a matter of deciding you want something different and putting thought and action behind it.

Net-worth view reduces the stress of monthly ups and downs.

One of the most common concerns for people who are leaving the grind behind is pay instability. What happens if I don't make sales one month? What if I am unable to collect from a customer? How will I pay my bills? How will I pay my mortgage?

A benefit of focusing on net worth is it smooths out the ups and downs of being a Grinder.

Think about driving a car. If your gauge is set to show feet per hour, the number will move wildly with minor changes in your car's speed. It will stress you out. If you consider feet-per-hour as your monthly income, miles-per-hour is your net worth. And since Grinders have variable income, it's important to smooth out your viewpoint to avoid stressing over the noise.

By viewing your financial situation primarily through the lens of net worth, you can modify habits before you actually quit your job. You can also make immediate changes and set yourself up to be financially ready to quit.

How do you track your net worth?

This is easy. List what you own and subtract out what you owe.

Common items people own. Add these up.

- Home. Grab its value from a real estate agent friend, www.zillow.com, or some other place. Write down the market value of the home.
- Cars. Head over to www.kbb.com to figure out the market value of your cars.
- Bank accounts. What is your balance in all accounts?
- Investment accounts. Do you have a 401K or other type of investment account?
- Other big, liquid assets.

Common items people owe. Subtract these.

- Mortgage
- Car loans
- Credit cards
- Tax burdens
- Other liabilities

The difference between the two is your net worth. If you owe more than you own, you have a negative net worth. If you own more than you owe, you have a positive net worth. By looking at your portfolio in this manner, you will automatically start taking actions to improve your net worth.

What are good tools for tracking your net worth?

Since I was committed to leaving the grind behind, I wanted a sophisticated tool that could easily track my net worth. I was looking for a tool that would automatically pull in account values, giving me net worth reports and visuals on demand. Personally, I chose Personal Capital (an online service that is free or paid depending on service level).

In addition, I enjoy the power of mentally and physically engaging in activities, so I also use simple graph paper to chart my net worth by hand.

How can you Change Your Net Worth?

Now that you're determined to measure your finances by net worth, it's time to drive change. You've seen the items that cause your net worth to go up and down. So you're off to a great start.

Step 1: Chart your net worth

The first step is level setting. Either with graphing paper or an online tool, chart your net worth.

Step 2: Set goals

Make sure your chart accounts for the future. Place stars on your future net-worth targets. Set a 90-day target, a 1-year target, and a 5-year target. Remember how powerful visualization and affirmations are. Putting your goals on paper leverages this power.

Step 3: Chart the trend

Review your net worth's history, plotting the past onto the same chart. How fast has it been changing? Project it into the future. If you just keep on going to work day-after-day, will you ever get where you want?

Step 4: Make changes

As Steven Covey would say, focus on the big rocks first, which is exactly what thinking about net worth does. You'll see the big levers you can pull to make big change.

Don't think about what will make small, imperceptible changes. This graph should shift your focus to the big drivers.

Here are some big items you can do while still a Cog:

- Buy or sell real estate, with a focus on cash flow
- Dig into your investments and move non-performing money around
- Start a debt repayment program
- Ensure you're taking advantage of eligible tax breaks
- Add new earnings that are scalable (more on this to come)

Step 5: Stay focused and take action

Look at your chart every day. Post that graph paper on the wall. Looking at it will give you ideas. Zoning out while looking at your graph will help feed your subconscious. Remember Grinder Jeeves? He loves to help with big tasks like growing net worth.

Step 6: Enlist help by focusing on net worth with your Mastermind Group

Still not sure what to do to move the needle? Have your Mastermind Group focus specifically on elevating each member's net worth. This is what I did. We all saw very significant increases in our net worth in short order.

What changes did I personally make to improve my net worth?

While preparing to quit my job, I did the following:

- Started a Mastermind Group focused on net worth.
- Sold my house and bought a better one. I cashed in on appreciation and leveraged a low down payment and low interest rates. I bought a home at below market value. My net worth instantly grew and has continued to jump. I partnered with a real estate agent who was also an ace investor. He helped me make this play.
- Saved more, especially as lumps of money came along (bonuses, taxes, etc...). This one, in particular, made me feel very comfortable about leaving the grind behind. I figured out how much padding I wanted and hit that goal.

- Made certain lifestyle changes that resulted in lower spending. You can see some of these details in the prior chapter on freeing up time and money.
- Became generally very deliberate about taking actions that would lead to an improved net worth.

What were my net-worth results?

After around 5 years of a fairly stagnant net worth, I focused my actions on it. As a result, I increased my net worth by 42% in 6 months (and this is before I left the grind behind). Awesome.

I targeted more initially and didn't hit that goal until 4 months later. But was I discouraged? Not at all. That's the beauty of big goals.

So not only was this an incredible improvement in my net worth, it was enough for me to feel financially confident enough to quit my job.

As this has played out, my net worth has continued to sky rocket. Within 1.5 years of leaving the grind behind, my net worth had more than doubled. And that's saying something: as a Cog, I was already ahead of the curve for my age. This was a significant change.

So much for startup failure. My net worth has continued to grow faster than I expected, putting many of my initially crazy goals right in sight. Focusing on the right gauge can do the same for you.

Grinders are Ruthless about Scalability

Now that you have a good sense of net worth, it's time to discuss the money magic that Grinders care about creating: scalability.

If you achieve a breakthrough in results, do you also receive a breakthrough in pay? The answer to that question is a quick test to determine if you're a Cog or a Grinder. It's the question you should ask yourself with every new business opportunity.

Think about what is really limited in life: time—not money. Therefore if you tie your money to time, you will artificially limit your money. If you earn a salary, you limit your earnings. If you leave the grind behind and run a business where you just charge an hourly consulting fee, sorry—you're still a Cog. Your earnings are tied to your time. Getting into the mindset of detaching money from time is what scalability is all about.

Scalability is about putting in approximately the same amount of effort, whether you sell 10 or 10,000 of something.

Every time you get an opportunity to make new money, figure out a way to attach scalability to it.

Let me give you a current example from my own life. I am working on marketing a new service that will flourish if the right partnership develops. It is a fairly low-risk endeavor for me, as it requires just a subset of my time. In exchange, I am receiving a moderate consultant base pay. As a side bonus, this gives me an opportunity to try out many of the marketing techniques I have learned. I get to put those ideas to the test with a big audience. Based on these benefits alone, this is a good deal for me.

But, there's more to this situation. This project is young. It has the potential to grow massively. It's well funded and has sharp leadership. It has the potential to scale. This is why I was attracted to it.

So, when it came time for me to negotiate with this organization, I could have taken a higher fixed-consulting fee. But, given the benefits inherent in the work and the fact that it may grow explosively, I chose to charge a lower fee *and* a percent of growth for deals I brought. I attached scalability.

If this goes as planned, it will generate many millions for the company I represent. Since I earn a percentage of the deal, I will also make a massive amount of money. It's win-win. This is how millionaires are forged.

I go for opportunities like this. These are gauge-needle movers and allow me to attach scalability but with minimal risk. As you transition from being a Cog to a Grinder, you'll want to shift your earnings more and more toward this type of construct.

Is scalability just sales?

Don't take this example to mean that I am saying you need to be a salesperson. It's really about finding a systematic way to deliver value to a lot of people. In my example, I was able to work a deal to touch millions of customers through a single arrangement.

You may also reach many potential customers through Internet marketing or releasing a book. The point is to find ways to touch many people and profit in a variable manner.

1. I put myself in a position to grow with whatever I touch. Apart from the potential for my income to scale, there are a few other benefits:I get more work. Companies love it when you put your money where your mouth is and you offer to benefit relative to your performance, which lowers their risk.

2. I enjoy the work more and become more devoted. If I know that my reward is scalable relative to what I do, then I'm that much more excited to be involved.

3. It sets me up to receive a windfall. And I can set myself up over and over. This gets back to one of the very first concepts discussed in this book—setting yourself up to hit bases-loaded home runs.

Is this the description of a salesperson? Perhaps. But I consider it just being savvy with both business and money in general.

With all of that said, let me be clear—if you create something of value, you have to sell it. Having an awesome product or service that no one knows about doesn't make you a Grinder. Every Grinder must be a salesperson.

The "If you build it, they will come" mentality will almost certainly result in failure. You do need to learn how to passionately connect your value with people in a scalable manner.

Cash flow and scalability

Another term you will hear as you become a Grinder is "cash flow." Scalability and cash flow go hand-in-hand. Cash flow looks at the money an asset earns for you. So just like with scalability, cash flow is all about separating money from time.

Cash flow is typically expressed as money you earn on a monthly basis, typically from an investment and net of costs. The simplest example of a cash-flowing asset is a rental property. If you buy a home and have $900 per month in costs but can rent it out for $1,650, your cash flow is $750 each month.

Cash-flowing assets are often scalable. Put more money in, get more money out. They're money machines. Going back to the rental property example, you could provide housing for one or 100 people. If you have the right property management systems in place, renting properties has nothing to do with your time. Time doesn't limit you, therefore it's scalable.

Whereas net worth is about impacting your balance sheet, cash flow is about impacting your income statement. Having scalability means you have the ability to explode both.

Alright, you should now have a good idea about how to think about money. The next chapter will dive into the best scalable ways to make money as a Grinder.

Grinder
Summary

1. If you're worried about money, you don't have a Grinder's mindset yet. Time is limited, not money.
2. Grinders focus on net worth and scalability.

3. Annual salary increases are for Cogs. Once you focus on net worth, you'll realize a miniscule 5% annual raise doesn't really do anything.

4. A key benefit of focusing on net worth is it smooths out the ups and downs of being a Grinder.

5. Change your net worth by:
    a. Charting your net worth.
    b. Setting future net worth goals.
    c. Charting your past net worth.
    d. Taking action and making day-to-day changes.
    e. Using net worth as a key metric of your Mastermind Group.

6. Making scalable earnings means huge windfalls.

7. As you start leaving the grind behind, offer to work on a percentage-earned basis. You'll get more deals, be more devoted, and have the chance to hit it big.

8. Cash flow is an important concept when it comes to scalability. It is about earning money from your assets (rentals), rather than relying on appreciation of value (stocks).

9. Want to learn all about scalability? Read *The Millionaire Fastlane* by MJ Demarco.

Grinder Action:
Chart Your Net Worth

Find a net-worth tracking tool that works for you. It may be best to keep it simple and grab a piece of graphing paper. If you're more computer-oriented, sign up for something like Mint or Personal Capital.

Track your net worth monthly. Plot it back in time several years to see how things have changed. Set goals for the future. Set a 90-day, 1-year, and 5-year target.

Grinder Habit:
Devote Mastermind Group Time to
Net Worth and Scalability

Leverage the power of multiple minds to find opportunities to improve your collective net worth numbers. Be transparent with your Mastermind Group by telling them your actual net worth number.

Learn about scalability and cash flow. Each person can find a different resource and report back to the group. Collectively work on creative ideas that improve your earning capacity.

CHAPTER 16

Make Money Easier

Alright, now that you have how Grinders think about money, it's time to dive into a Grinder Money Framework that will put you on the path of parlaying that knowledge into income.

Specifically, we'll look at the best ways to make money and the concept of earning multiple income streams. The subsequent chapters will then dive into practical ideas and methods.

The 5 Characteristics of the Best Ways to Make Money

1. Repeatability and models

Sure, winning the lottery sounds like a great way to make money. But what are the chances of doing it? What are the chances of repeating it and making it a consistent money building model?

Rather than looking for one-time events, we should look for ways to *consistently* make money. We want repeatable, scalable models.

In fact, if you want to minimize risk, until you have significant success in a particular venture, the best approach is *not* to innovate. Grinders are big on the concept of models. Follow a model. Follow a proven path to success. Start where others who have exceeded in your area have left off, then follow their model and add your own enhancements.

For example, if you want to invest in real estate, there are good and bad models. Find a good model and execute. Don't spend your time inventing your own way of doing things. Don't waste your time and money trialing ideas. Choose a method that succeeds and then execute flawlessly.

By emphasizing execution, you greatly reduce your risk while simultaneously improving your speed to success. Models are a key part of how I quickly began making money after I left the grind behind. I plugged in to the models of successful people (my mentors) rather than starting from scratch.

2. Passive income and scalability

This is a biggie. If you don't need to be involved in the process, income can grow without your direct time and input.

Passive income builds on the concept of "repeatability." If you have a repeatable process for making money that doesn't rely on your time, it can either be automated or outsourced, which largely removes you from the process. And if you don't need to be involved in the day-to-day, then you truly have a money machine. Further, you have freedom to pursue other interests.

Here's another goodie: passive income is rewarded by the IRS. Seriously. Passive income is taxed less, which is a significant bonus.

3. Tax advantaged

Speaking of taxes, when you make a good amount of earned income, you may find rising taxes to be an issue. It is common for 60% of your income to be consumed by standard expenses and bills. Then another 35% goes to tax. Will that allow you to build wealth and become a millionaire quickly? Not at all.

However, the government offers tax-break rewards for certain situations and income streams. These sources of income are another key component in determining the best way to make money.

Let's look at an example of how impactful taxes are:

Standard Cog Income

- Income of $100,000
- Personal Expenses & Bills of 60%
- Tax rate of 25%
- Money that can be saved: $1,250 per month

Tax-Advantaged Grinder Income

- Income of $100,000
- Expenses of 60%
- Tax rate of 5%
- Money that can be saved: $2,917 per month

That's a huge difference! What could you do with an extra $20,000 per year? Viewed another way, you could earn much less as a Grinder and still maintain the same spending and savings rate you had as a Cog. That's huge and a major safety net right there.

If you plan your expenses right, you can get by on much less money. So if you have a rough start or a bad few months as a Grinder, the impact won't be an issue.

There are several people in my circle who live *completely* off passive income. They live great lives of which most would be envious.

Their income, however, is surprisingly low relative to what you'd expect. And it's low relative to the lifestyle they are living. Earning income in a tax-advantaged manner has allowed them to get much farther with every penny.

The lesson is to make sure you understand your tax implications well. Earn money in tax-advantaged ways. Save money in tax-advantaged ways.

A good CPA will benefit you massively. If you find one that understands the concerns and lifestyle of a Grinder, hire them—they will pay for themselves many times over.

4. No limits

A significant problem with a W2 job is you likely have some serious limits on your earning potential. Do you make $60,000 now? If you work hard for years and sacrifice yourself for the company, can you set yourself up for a $120,000 salary? Will that really get you where you want to be? When will you become a millionaire if you follow this path?

As I looked at the commitment top management gave to their companies and compared that to the compensation they received, I quickly decided I needed to find an alternate path.

The real answer is to look for ways to make money that have no ceiling. This is how people make millions.

If you make $1 from something you sell to a million people, the math is pretty simple. What happens if you can make $10 per unit? What if that item continues to sell long after you stop putting direct effort into it? That can happen with books, software, and much more. This is the beauty of scalability. And it simply cannot be achieved at a W2 job, no matter how good or committed you are.

So look for big-audience options. Reach a lot of people and you will eliminate ceilings.

5. Low barriers

If you already have massive amounts of money and tons of unique knowledge, there are probably numerous ways for you to enter high-barrier fields and capitalize. However, if we're trying to determine the best way to repeatedly make money as you become a Grinder, we want the barriers to entry to be *low*.

This means you shouldn't need a huge amount of upfront money. And it also means you should be able to learn the game relatively quickly.

People disagree with me on this. They will say low barriers to entry means you'll have to compete with everyone. But does everyone have your drive? Is everyone a Grinder? Heck no.

With the right motivation, you can almost always stand out from the crowd in a significant way. Just because something is easy doesn't mean most people will do it successfully. And of those who do, what percent is really committed to doing what it takes to be a success?

If you enter a low-barrier arena, you stand out by playing the game better than your competition. If you enter a high-barrier arena, you'll burn a significant amount of time and money just figuring out if you can even play.

I can rely on myself to push harder than the next guy, so low-entry barriers allow me to get in with minimal risk. You just need to grind—that's it.

I've seen this in practice many times in my work with start-ups. There is a clear division between people who believe they need to position themselves in high-barrier areas and people who are fine going into low-barrier areas.

Simply put, I have consistently seen much more failure in high-barrier arenas. Players here burn much more cash, require much more (expensive) expertise, and have more distant horizons before profitability *might* be reached. This means they go through cash for a long time before even knowing if they will make money.

The lesson has been clear to me: go with low-barrier activities. You can always offer a fresh perspective, work harder, and maybe even ride the coat-tails of a competitor whose audience is ready for something new.

Now, if you use these principles to make millions, by all means, chase something crazy big. But keep it simple to start.

Multiple Income Streams

Now that you know the various characteristics of making money smartly, it's time to put things together and add income streams before you quit your W2 job. This reduces the risk from leaving the stability of Cog life.

I quickly learned that Grinders in my network shared a common practice: earning multiple income streams. As I met people who were extraordinarily successful in one area, I found they were also making money elsewhere. They were playing the money game smartly.

"Diversified" is a term you commonly hear thrown around. Cogs worry about having a diversified portfolio, a problem they fix by investing in mutual funds and just the right blend of stocks and bonds. Grinders don't consider this to be diversification. Diversification is real income coming from multiple avenues.

Types of income

Before we dive into how to build multiple income streams, I'll cover the various types of income to consider, including hourly, salary, results-based, and passive.

Ultimately, passive income backed by "results-based" earned income is the way to build wealth. The more you are exposed to these types of income, the more their power becomes apparent and the less risk you'll see. This is due to their inherent scalability. Your goal is to transition your income this direction over time.

Of course, *most* people prefer hourly and salaried pay for their earned income. This is understandable. We have obligations, families, and other basics that we want to ensure are cared for month-to-month. Most of us are conditioned to go out and get a "nice, steady job." These are the reasons we so easily accept being a Cog.

But, as a Grinder, you know hourly and salary income is limited, is tied directly to your time, and is heavily taxed. That sounds much riskier to me. Here's a look at the alternatives:

1. Results-Based Income

Results-based income is commonly commission income. This means you are paid based on accomplishing a particular goal. Oftentimes, you are paid a percentage of the income a business generates.

This type of pay is low risk for the company paying you. You only make money if the company makes money. Because of this, companies have no problem paying you massive amounts if you deliver massive results. In fact, top sales people are often among the highest paid people at a company.

Results-based pay is the easiest way to sell your knowledge, build experience, and generate additional income. If you don't make a real difference, you don't get paid. Because of this, it's easy to get results-based pay gigs when you're starting out.

2. Passive Income

We've talked a lot about passive income already, but let me provide a bit more color in the context of this chapter.

Passive income is income you receive with very little or no effort from you. Examples include lease income, royalties, and earnings you make from other people's efforts.

Generally, passive income is the long-term result of up-front effort. You spend time writing a book and earn money from it thereon out. If you buy a rental property, you put time in searching, rehabbing, and buying all upfront. Then you earn income with minimal ongoing effort. If you build a website, the same principle applies.

Because it is about upfront effort, passive income lends itself quite well to leaving the grind behind. While still at your W2 job, you can take time to work on a book, software, or other project. The income you earn provides ongoing padding for you, reducing the risk of losing W2 income.

Your Time vs Your Pay

Both passive income and results-based earned income offer a particular advantage over traditional hourly and salaried pay: your time is not linked to your pay. Time is no longer a limiting factor. When you separate time from pay, you may spend large amounts of upfront time, with no immediate pay and no promise of pay. However, your time...and therefore earnings...may scale.

Once you get an income stream up and running, you can move it into maintenance mode and begin working on your next.

How to Transition to Passive and Results-Based Income

In order to avoid jumping in feet first and losing your house, I recommend phasing in both passive income and results-based income. Phasing is a key component of this book's strategy and will help you become a Grinder with minimal risk.

Phasing doesn't need to take years. You can aggressively transition your income types. As you do, you will learn a lot about how to add value to other people's lives, how to become comfortable without a steady paycheck, and how to win at the game of money. How to be a Grinder.

To transition effectively, you will want to ensure you are tracking your income types each month:

1. Total income
2. Hourly or salaried income
3. Results-based income
4. Passive income

The goal here is to see your percentages shifting month-over-month away from hourly and salaried income.

My Income Transition Results

- To give you an idea of how this can pan out, here are my results. Within 1.5 years of quitting my 6-figure salaried job, I accomplished the following:Doubled my total income

- Created 6 income streams, with 3 more in the works
- Had an average split of just about 33% base, 33% results- based, and 33% passive
- Was working *less* than I was when I was at my W2 job

Monthly, these percentages are shifting toward passive income, which is a prime goal of mine. My objective then is pretty simple. When a new opportunity comes by, I seek out results-based income. That's how the percentages move. Additionally, now that I have a steady base that keeps me comfortable, I continue to invest both my time and money in passive investments and projects.

Grinder Summary

1. When considering how best to make money, look for 5 characteristics in your opportunity:
    a. Repeatability and models
    b. Passive income and scalability
    c. Tax advantages
    d. No limits
    e. Low barriers
2. Earning money through multiple income streams is a key way to transition from Cog to Grinder and minimize your risk. New income streams should be results-based and/or passive.
3. Track your income monthly and bucket it as follows, watching allocations shift as you become a Grinder:

a. Total income

b. Hourly or salaried income

c. Results-based income

d. Passive income

Grinder Action:
Brainstorm New Income Streams

The action for this chapter is pretty simple. Sit down and list out at least 20 ways you could make money on the side. Evaluate each of these against the 5 characteristics of the best ways to make money, giving each idea a score.

If you're having trouble thinking of ideas, go back to Section 1 of this book and sync back up with your purpose statement. Next, get with your Mastermind Group and mentors to jointly brainstorm.

Once you have ideas, seek input on them. But be careful! Most Cogs will tell you reasons *not* to do something. While prudence is important, Cogs don't know your drive and willingness to do what it takes to become a Grinder. So instead of relying on feedback from Cogs, seek it out from Grinders: your mentor and Mastermind Group.

Once you feel you have a few potential ideas to run with, get started, even if it's just on the side.

Grinder Habit:
Track Your Income Streams

You're already tracking your net worth on a monthly basis, so now you'll simply add a breakdown of your income and how it is earned. Categorize your monthly income as:

- Total income
- Hourly or salaried income
- Results-based income
- Passive income

Plot this over time so you can monitor the change and make corrections as needed. Also write out some stated goals and affirmations to make it very clear where you want your income to trend.

This is your last Grinder Habit. The chapters going forward will give you insight into how to begin building these buckets. It's all action from here.

CHAPTER 17

Initial Grinder Income Streams

Alright, now that you know how Grinder money works, it's time to go get some.

Adding new streams of income gets you into the flow of being a Grinder. It gives you financial padding, which makes quitting your job an easier choice. And once you see results, leaving the grind behind becomes believable.

Here, I'll talk about adding income streams and multiplying existing ones.

Ten Starter Income Streams and Multipliers

Following is a list I personally leveraged as I transitioned to a Grinder. These items were recommended to me by my coach at the time and are fairly common across other successful people in my network. These are a mix of ideas that can multiply your current income or allow you to add additional streams. Each aligns with the money characteristics from the last chapter.

If it seems they will take a lot of money, you're probably over-estimating and simply need to better educate yourself.

By the way, if you'd like a great, easy system for tracking your new money streams, read *Profit First* by Mike Michalowicz. It will also help ensure you grow these streams in a way that ensures profitability.

Ask your employer for results-based income

If you are working for someone, either as W2 or as a contractor, exchange some of your base pay for results-based pay.

Even if you work at a corporate job (shackled by "HR policy"), you may be surprised by the willingness of your organization to take you up on your request to change your pay model. I have successfully made this change in several jobs, and here is my recommended approach:

1. Identify the key metric you're hired to improve.
2. Propose a pay structure where you receive a portion of your pay as a *steady* base. This is less than what you make today.
3. Propose the other portion be tied to the result of that metric, which is now your *variable* pay.

Determine a factor for that metric, so that as the metric improves, you receive higher pay. Of course, if the metric goes down, you receive less pay. As an alternative, you can seek bonuses at certain achievement milestones. For this proposal to fly, your model sum should be *less* than your existing pay at the metric's current state. In other words, you're taking a hit if things stay the same. This shows the company that you're committed to results and you only benefit if you truly improve the business. It's win-win.

Asking for pay changes from smaller businesses is easy. In fact, most small businesses will prefer results-based pay. But if you work at a corporate job and are not sure how to request a pay change like this, you may just need the right connections and advocates within your company—go back to the chapter on mentoring if you need help with this.

Improving sales is the easiest and most common approach for results-based pay. But this concept can also be applied to almost any metric, such as customer satisfaction, productivity, expense reduction, and more.

Switching to this pay structure will give you the gift of time. No longer will you feel compelled to work a certain number of hours. Rather, you work for results. Some weeks, you'll be able to deliver the results without much direct effort. Some weeks you'll put in more blood and sweat. Delinking time from pay allows you to pursue other income streams and work toward being a Grinder.

2. Start with consulting

For many people, the first step to leaving the grind behind is becoming a consultant. You can consult on the side, building a portfolio and some business savvy prior to quitting. It allows you to get your feet wet.

However, most people approach consulting from a Cog's perspective. What I am instead suggesting is to take consulting gigs on a percentage, results-based basis—not an hourly pay basis. If you make a big impact on someone's results, get rewarded accordingly. If you don't, learn from your mistakes and apply them going forward.

Apart from setting yourself up to earn more, there is another distinction to this: you're more likely to get hired. It's always tough to get your first few clients. But if you put your money where your mouth is, you reduce the risk for your client. You get paid if you deliver. It forces you to add real value.

Should you find consulting works very well for you, you can outsource pieces of the work and begin separating yourself from the process and creating a true money machine. More on this to come.

3. Hitchhike on someone else's grind

Do you or your Mastermind Group know someone who is a Grinder? Perhaps you can consult for them and fill a skill gap. Or perhaps they want something more—they want the mental equity a partner can bring.

Indeed, much like many businesses start as a partnership because the owners need to pool money, mental partnerships also arise.

Starting a business is hard work! You need brain power, strategic thought, manpower to get things done, and a broad network of people. Many Grinders welcome a partner, whether financially or otherwise.

If someone else is taking on capital risk, you have to figure out what you provide and how much that is worth. Maybe you can tag onto a business for 10% of profits by contributing certain work and strategic insight. Maybe you can negotiate an escalating percentage, whereby you make a larger percent as the company grows.

The point of this idea is simply to get talking to your network. See if there are opportunities. I earn money like this from a couple of businesses whose growth I impact, and it is one of my most enjoyable revenue stream types.

4. The answer is never "I don't have enough time!"

"I don't have enough time to do that" should never be an excuse. If I ever find myself working too many hours, I simply pause and write down what I can push off to someone else. That is how you grow—you remove yourself as a limiting factor. Letting go also gives you more of your time back.

Are you choosing to do activities that prevent you from making the highest and best use of your time? Instead of saying you "I don't have time" say "I need help." If you get assistance, you free up time to do the right things. And assistance has math magic in its favor. Here's how…

Doing everything yourself is a Cog behavior and it locks you into being a Cog. Outsourcing everything is a Grinder behavior. It allows you to focus on growing your business opportunities and living the life you design. So start early and get in the habit of having assistance.

Nearly all successful small business owners I know have assistants, and they hire them *early.* In fact, one of my top business coaches recommends that as soon as you make 6 figures, you should hire an assistant. He has seen this level-jump his results time and again.

This is the case *even if* you are a regular W2 employee. If your employer won't hire you an assistant, hire your own. Seriously. I have.

In fact, I recommend hiring assistants even earlier than the 6-figure mark–especially since you can get outstanding interns for free.

You don't have to hire someone for 40 hours per week. You can find people willing to do just a few hours of work each week, which can offload a ton from your shoulders.

So how does hiring someone help generate another income stream? The math may surprise you. If you earn the equivalent of $50 per hour and can pay someone $15 per hour to do a subset of that work, you will be able to earn the equivalent of $85 per hour. That's $100 – $15, which is $85 per hour…not $35 per hour as people may mistakenly think.

	You Earnings	Outsourcing Expense	Net Income
Without Assistant	$50/hour	$0	$50/hour
With Assistant	$50/hour	$15/hour	$85/hour

Why is this? If you work 20 hours per week at $50 per hour and have someone who can take 10 hours per week off your plate, you can then apply your skills to earn your value in another way for those extra 10 hours. Therefore, for the cost of $15, you free up 10 hours. That is why the math is $100 - $15, not $50 - $15.

Assistants give you the gift of the scarcest resource: time. Personally, I have been shocked by how much more I can earn when I have an assistant in place.

It makes me happier too. I hire assistants *who like doing the work I don't*. The result is they are vastly more efficient with the work I give them. That annoying filing and bookkeeping that takes me 4 hours to complete? It only takes them 1 hour. Now my earnings math is even better. I pay them $15 to free up 4 hours of my time.

Do you think this won't work in your W2 Cog job? That thinking will keep you a Cog. Keep reading.

Here are a few tasks you can hire an assistant or intern to do:

1. Perform routine and repeatable tasks, like building reports, entering data, filing, organizing, etc. If you have tasks that are time-intensive and repeatable, you shouldn't spend your time doing them.

2. Tasks you don't like doing. If you don't like coordinating schedules, booking travel, logging miles, doing mailers, or whatever—give those items to an assistant. This allows you to focus on what you like and find creatively challenging tasks.

3. Research. Oftentimes, you need to spend hours researching to make smart, accurate, up-to-date recommendations at your job. Having someone research and summarize for you can offload huge amounts of time. I use this method to have people start writing articles for me in my various lines of business. This is how it's possible for me to create content for 5 different businesses. People do the research, start the content, then I finish it off. Handling just one of these businesses on my own would push me over the edge. An assistant lets me scale.

4. If you cannot find something work-related because you'd be breaking corporate rules, think about tasks within your personal life to offload. If you're excited to start a new blog, but are bogged down by household chores…get assistance at home to clean, mow, or prep meals. You can find assistance in many areas of life for much cheaper than you may expect. Neighborhood kids love to mow for a few bucks. And if your earning power is greater than the cost, it's worth it.

Again, if you think cost is an issue, get over that. You have the math to show the value. But also consider that you can often bring on an intern for free. You will need to provide mentoring in return, but that's a bonus in my mind.

Alternatively, you can pay your assistants in a results-based manner. If they impact your results, everyone wins. Find someone who is looking to become a Grinder and have them help you out in areas you're weak. For example, I'm weak at editing. I have a friend who is breaking into editing. It's a perfect match, and I can pay him a percentage of sales. Simple and exciting for both of us.

5. Add income by making money off of someone else's effort

Very similar to hiring an assistant, you may be in position to make money in one of the best possible ways: through someone else's effort.

Though this sounds like hiring an assistant, you are generally hiring skilled labor and letting them do the bulk of the work. You then leverage your expertise to do final oversight and ensure quality is up to your standards.

Where assistants compliment your skillsets, making money off others is generally done more directly within your own skillset.

It is standard to pay a more junior employee 50% less than what you charge for the job. This means you increase your total billable time and improve your margins.

As already mentioned, there is no such thing as being *too busy*. You either need to hire an assistant or make money by billing for someone else's time.

There are countless ideas in this space. Start doing research on different ways people make money off of someone else. A few thoughts:

1. Scour The Fastlane Forums (thefastlaneforum.com/community) or similar sites to see how you can use people in low-cost geographies to execute on your ideas. You might be shocked by how much money some Grinders are able to make doing simple things like publishing other people's writing, drop-shipping, and more.

2. If you're already in business for yourself but don't make Grinder-level money, get started. For example, if you're a plumber working for yourself, hire a junior plumber. Send them to your simpler jobs. Bill at your rate, but pay them at a junior rate.

3. If you're leveraging some of your experience to offer consulting, there may be someone else you can bring in to work directly with clients. This makes them different than an assistant but provides similar results.

6. Invest in a business owned by a friend

Stocks are hard to valuate and are subject to many outside forces that are next to impossible to predict. Look no further than the blindfolded, dart-throwing monkey experiment done by Princeton University. The study's author Burton Malkiel concluded "a blindfolded monkey throwing darts at a newspaper's financial pages could select a portfolio that would do just as well as one carefully selected by experts."

> "'Malkiel was wrong,' stated Rob Arnott, CEO of Research Affiliates, while speaking at the IMN Global Indexing and ETFs conference earlier this month. 'The monkeys have done a much better job than both the experts and the stock market.'
>
> "In their yet-to-be-published article, the company randomly selected 100 portfolios containing 30 stocks from a 1,000 stock universe. They repeated this processes every year, from 1964 to 2010, and tracked the results. The process replicated 100 monkeys throwing darts at the stock pages each year. Amazingly, on average, 98 of the 100 monkey portfolios beat the 1,000 stock capitalization weighted stock universe each year."
>
> ~ Ferri, Rick – 'Any Monkey Can Beat the Market' ~

Why do I bring this up? To show that the risk and speed at which stocks make money make this an unacceptable Grinder income stream. And while day trading may seem attractive, I have yet to meet anyone who consistently earns money by doing so. Stocks should be part of your long-term investment strategy, but I cannot recommend them as a Grinder income stream.

Whereas stocks are hard to valuate, it's possible to valuate companies you are close to. So if you don't yet have your own great business idea, you can work your network. Reach out and see who is already pursuing a dream. Interview them. Understand what they're trying to do.

You can much more easily validate the success potential of someone within your network than a publicly traded company. In this sense, businesses within your network can be valuated and may provide great income potential.

Further, people within your network are likely to be interested in your investment. They may offer you benefits or more rights than you'd get by simply buying a bigger company's stock.

Of course the downside is risk of catastrophic failure, but that's why you investigate and perform due diligence. I recommend the due diligence be done primarily on the business owner(s). Many factors change with businesses, but if you have the right leader in a small but growing company, you have a good investment.

In fact, when considering an investment, entrepreneur and investment expert Howard Tullman evaluates his investments based on *"the strength of the leader's traits, namely preparation, perspiration, perseverance, principles, and passion."*

Doesn't that sound easier to value than the vast array of factors that determine a stock's price?

On top of everything I do, I invest in several businesses owned by close friends. I know their drive. I know whether or not they'll do what it takes to be a success. I know in whom to invest.

Investing in a business will generate truly passive income for you, unless you decide to participate in the operations. Depending on your investment, you may also consider becoming a board member. This will give you further insight into running a business and becoming a Grinder.

7. Turn your interests and hobbies into income

If there is something you're good at and have expertise with, there is almost certainly a way to translate it into dollars. In fact, one of the most satisfying things you can do is share your passions with others in a way that adds value to their lives.

I should note there are experts who recommend *not* following your passions as a way to make money. While it's true you need to line up with a market need to make money, what I'm suggesting is a bit different.

This is an opportunity to take something you're interested in and use it to learn some of the facets of being a Grinder. And unless you have a super-odd passion, chances are there are others out there that have your passion too.

Further, you don't need to be an end-all, be-all expert. Many people are just starting out on interests every day. Certainly there is something you can help people start.

Take your interests online

A common way to do this is via a blog. The barriers to entry are very low, you can reach a very large audience, and you have the chance to generate truly passive income. Make no mistake though, there is an art and science to making money online. But it can be very lucrative and rewarding. The skills you learn to stand out online will almost certainly be needed once you become a full-time Grinder.

In fact, even if you're not yet sure how you'll monetize what you know, I suggest you get going anyway just for the value of what you'll learn. Begin writing articles, creating videos, or otherwise expressing yourself creatively. This will help you find an audience and refine your message, all while creating a wealth of information that can later be packaged as a product or book. This jives well with transitioning from your Cog job, as it is something you can do on the side and will probably enjoy.

Of course, the best option is to start with something to sell and build a presence around that concept. However, that can delay you. Many of us don't know what we want to sell. And it may take a significant amount of time or money to ready something for sale. By confining yourself to creating only if you have something to sell, you risk remaining a Cog forever.

So instead, get started with something and worry about monetization later. You'll begin making new connections, discovering new ideas, and finding problems in the market place you can tackle. Your audience will tell you what they want. It's amazing what "getting yourself out there" can do in terms of teaching you how to make money.

The first website I started while still in my W2 job sucked. The content was marginal, it wasn't focused, and it had no real purpose for existing. However, I am still extremely glad I did it. I gained so many valuable skills and connections. I simply wouldn't be a Grinder today if it wasn't for that site.

Take your interests local

If going online isn't your forte, you can do something similar at a local level: mentor and teach. Teaching can scale quite well. You can mentor 1 person, then offer a 10-person class, and ultimately pack a conference room. You get to charge by the head.

While the income isn't passive, you are paid in a results-based manner. And ultimately, the materials you create will be easy to put together into a manual, book, or online course that will become truly passive income. You'll find many local centers that make teaching classes simple.

What's important here is you're leveraging something youenjoy to break out of the standard grind and explore ways to live life on your terms.

For example, do you know a lot about dreams? Perhaps you can offer a dream interpretation class. Whatever your interest, there is almost certainly someone out there who would like to learn about that interest. They are just starting out and are a blank slate. Many people are happy to pay for that human touch to get themselves started.

During the journey, you'll pick up a lot of great lessons related to marketing, sales, and operations. You probably need to form a company, like an LLC. Doing so is very emblematic and empowering. Starting with your interests is a simple and motivating approach.

By the way, I have a whole chapter coming up about getting online. So if this one piques your interest, keep reading for more info.

8. Sell options

I just told you *not* to invest in the stock market as a way to add an additional income stream. Specifically, don't expect to day trade your way out of your W2 job. Trading stocks takes a lot of time and attention while the markets are open. This can make it practically impossible for people working at a standard job.

There are numerous other challenges too. Trade commissions kill profits. Conflicting advice and a never-ending stream of gurus, tools, and platforms all ensure you'll spin your wheels, losing time and money while you're at it.

But none of those reasons are the real killers. There are systems and algorithms to beat the stock market. You'll simply never be able to beat the machines scalping the market while moving more coolly, calmly, and quickly than you. These mechanized trading platforms are run by the big companies and make it difficult—*I think impossible*—for an individual to win.

So what gives? Why am I recommending you sell options? Options offer certain low-risk vehicles that can deliver relatively steady income on a monthly basis. Further, the time required to monitor and manage trades is very low, thus making option-selling compatible with W2 jobs.

Specifically, I'm referring to selling "insurance." That means you operate your trades exactly in the same way insurance companies do. You sell protection against very low probability events.

There are many people who speculate by buying options that have a slim chance of ever being profitable. But if that option does work out, the buyer stands to make a decent amount of money. So the buyer has a *low probability of making a large amount of money*. These options are more about gambling than investing or running a business.

So what can a Grinder do? They can sell these options. Grinders take the opposite side of the trade: *a high probability of making a small amount of money...*over and over again. This is exactly how insurance companies do it.

While I've never met a consistently successful day trader, I do know people who consistently sell options successfully.

If you want to sell options, you must educate yourself and find a mentor. The principle is simple, but the execution takes specialized knowledge and training. Insurance companies are able to play this game because they have a good underwriting model. As an options seller, that is also what you need.

If selling options interests you, it is well worth your time to learn. It can absolutely be done while you are transitioning out of your W2 job. Do some research or if you'd like some recommendations, email me at justin@grindbehindbook.com.

9. Buy real estate

Alright, this one is a biggie. It deserves its own dedicated chapter...which is coming. But let me give you a primer here.

Real estate is insanely powerful and can become a career in and of itself. When I was first considering leaving the grind behind, the prospect of owning investment real estate sounded unreal. How would I get together enough money to buy additional real estate? How would I know how to buy correctly?

This barrier to entry bugged me because it was clear that a successful person I knew owned a lot of real estate. How did they get started?

As I began to ask and prod, my eyes opened. These real estate investors didn't necessarily have more money than me when they first started buying real estate. What I found out is they simply had more knowledge.

Don't let this happen to you. Don't let the large price tags on houses fool you—with the right expertise, real estate can become part of your earnings portfolio for much less than you may realize. I'll dive in with more depth in the coming chapter.

10. Think my list sucks? Consult your Mastermind Group.

The items I listed have been tried and true for me, but if they don't work for you for whatever reason, don't stop here. Don't be a Cog—keep pressing until you figure out how to become a Grinder. And remember you're not alone. This is exactly the sort of problem your Mastermind Group and mentor are here to solve for you.

So rather than being negative about my list, get brainstorming with your network and keep moving forward.

Grinder
Summary

1. Adding new streams of income gets you into the flow of being a Grinder. It gives you more financial padding

to make quitting your job an easier choice. It adds believability to leaving the grind behind.

2. Here are ideas to improve your income situation:
   a. Ask your employer for results-based income.
   b. Start consulting on the side.
   c. The answer is never "I don't have enough time!" Pay an assistant already.
   d. Add income by making money off of someone else, even if it's someone half-way around the world. e. Invest in a friend-owned business.
   e. Turn your interests and hobbies into income. g. Sell options.
   f. Buy real estate.
   g. Consult your Mastermind Group and mentor.
3. Don't assume you don't have enough money to take these steps. Most don't take capital on your part. And you're probably over-estimating the amount of money needed simply because you haven't educated yourself enough.
4. Read *Profit First* by Mike Michalowicz to learn how to best track your new income and keep it profitable.

Grinder Action: Make a Choice and Get Started

You've transitioned past the preparation part of this book. It's time to see what you're really made of. Are you really a Grinder?

If you've freed up time in your schedule based on prior actions in this book, you're at the point where you need to make that time productive.

Start by picking one of the ideas in the chapter. Or if none of them suits you, consult with your Mastermind Group for ideas. But pick something *this week.*

As a next step, brainstorm a list of at least 10 ways you can begin putting your ideas into action. Go back to the chapter on taking action. Map out what needs to be done, break it down, and start now.

Have a true heart-to-heart with yourself at this step. If you can't get going here, you might not have what it takes to be a Grinder.

CHAPTER 18

Make Money
With Your Expertise

While I already hit on Grinder consulting in the previous chapter, it deserves a deep dive of its own. Most Grinders I know got their start by consulting. It's generally the easiest first step and one you should seriously consider taking ASAP.

Did you know consultants generally make twice as much as their employee counterparts? If you make $40 per hour as a bookkeeper, you can probably charge $80 per hour as a consultant.

Why is this? Hiring employees is risky for companies. What if the employee doesn't work out? What if there isn't enough work? Not to mention benefits and other human resources overhead. With a consultant, it's easy to cut ties and companies can pay for just what they need, no more.

Also, consultancies tend to be more strategic in nature. Companies are able to bring in experts to help them get over obstacles or push to the next level. Because these engagements tend to be temporary, consultants can demand higher pay to compensate for their strategic value and also to offset the risk associated with the instability of the position.

The only real problem is it's easy to get consulting wrong. It's easy to mistakenly stay a Cog.

What Consulting Should You Provide?

While you're still in your Cog job, you can consult on the side. This gives you experience and clients and sets you up to be a Grinder. Most people don't think they have the expertise to be a consultant. But the reality is, if you've been doing something for a reasonable amount of time (say 2-3+ years), you should know plenty.

Start by doing a skills inventory. What specific skills have you developed over time? Which of those do you like? Which are you an ace at? Get specific and try to make a list of at least 20 skills you have.

Yeah, that's right. Make another list.

Once you have your list, think about which of those skills are not held or liked by many people. Then, see if any of those skills go for a high fee. Do some internet searching to get an idea of pricing.

If you can find something you're good at that normally costs a lot of money, you've found something you can use to break into being a Grinder.

For me, it was website design, online marketing, and telecom strategy.

How Do You Sell Your Service?

Now here's the thing—I don't want you to create a website, buy radio ads, and start competing with the big boys. This is a side gig designed to get you experience and get you in the corridor.

So, to get your first deals, leverage your network. Use your Mastermind Group and mentor.

Once you have someone you know who might benefit from your services, meet with them. Listen to their needs. Tell them you're in a transition and looking to build your portfolio. As such, you're willing to work in a non-traditional model. A *results*-based model.

Results-based pay only

Go back and review the best ways to make money and develop a framework around this. Make money for results. Reduce their risk and expense of hiring you. If you grow their business, you make more money...which they'll be delighted to pay you.

You could of course make less money this way, but you may also make a huge amount if you do it right. Either way, you've gained experience, exposure, and are living many of the ideals in this book.

Don't forget the metrics

If you're earning results-based pay, you are impacting some metric that leads to your pay going up or down. This number will also be important for your Grinder resume. You want to show the business impact you're making.

Get a snapshot of how that metric (revenue for example) has performed for the last year, six months, and whatever other timeframes are relevant.

Keep a detailed log of that number going forward. Use it in your personal marketing. If there are other accessible numbers, use those too.

This is how I'm able to list accomplishments such as:

- 81% reduction in marketing cost/acquisition via scientific advertising.
- 37% year-over-year increase in revenue base.
- 82%+ year-over-year growth in revenue.
- 640% increase in online sales.

Negotiate, Negotiate, Re-Negotiate

Once you get in with someone and start delivering results, it's time to re-evaluate your terms. It's likely at the time you created an agreement, neither of you really had a good feel for how the engagement would play out. As such, renegotiation after an initial honeymoon period is welcomed by both sides.

If the company is doing well and you're jiving, it's great to earn even higher results-based pay. Drop any retainer or hourly base and go purely on results. Perhaps it's time to deepen not only pay, but the relationship. Is it possible to become a true partner?

If you don't like the work or the company, ask for more money. Make it worth your while. Do this especially if you're not learning much.

Avoid Cog Pitfalls

When consulting, watch out for some common mistakes. First, don't charge *just* an hourly rate. While you can charge a solid fee, you're not really achieving your goal of being a Grinder. And since you're just starting out, you probably don't have the muscle to demand high fees. Make your engagement low risk for the company, but give yourself upside.

Second, don't do it all yourself. Start handing off work. If there is any routine or repetition in the work you do, have someone else do it for you. If you can charge $150 per hour and have someone do some of that work for $15 an hour, you may be cracking the code for creating a money machine.

Third, don't advertise your services. Stick to your network and extended network. People need a degree of trust in your services. If you're spending your time selling to a cold audience, you're going to get distracted and waste a lot of time and money.

However, if you're starting to do well based on your network, you may have the blueprint for a money machine. Here's when to consider making it a business:

1. You have documented success metrics.
2. You have clients willing to vouch for you.
3. You are able to hand work off to assistants. *It's scalable.*

If you have a true money machine, then start breaking my rules here and get on with developing your business with full focus.

My Adventures in Consulting

When I was ready to leave the grind behind, I left my nice job to become a real estate agent. Why? I knew real estate agents who were making insane amounts of money while only working a few hours. I also knew the power of real estate investing and wanted to get in the game.

But the problem is I also knew the average real estate agent makes something like $20 grand annually…that's not going to fly. So I needed to figure out how to do it properly.

Leveraging my network

First, I found a mentor. He was someone in my network making big money with his real estate license. He had rentals. He did flips. He had a team doing sales and running the details and day-to-day for him. He was pursuing his own interests. A true Grinder.

As it turned out, he was at a pivot point himself. He just bought the business from his dad but had little interest in running the team. He needed someone with operations and management experience, but those people were expensive. He had a problem.

Also, he was getting tired of real estate and wanted to work on building a web empire. But he didn't have a lot of the technical skills needed to get his ideas in front of the world.

Their problem, my opportunity

This was a major opportunity for me. I quit my job and moved so I could sit next to him daily. I would see firsthand how he made money and invested. I'd plug into his network. I could shortcut my path to making it big in real estate.

And he needed help that I was perfectly suited for. I could consult for him. We agreed he would pay me a monthly consulting fee to guide the team and handle some of the general profit and loss management. I'd also help architect and handle the technical end of his website.

But, I made a mistake. I took this work on with a flat monthly fee. Too bad I didn't have this book to read beforehand.

Renegotiation time

Well, both his real estate business and online business began taking off. His needs grew, so it was a perfect time for us to renegotiate. I kept a certain base pay, but also added results-based components. I'd earn the majority of my money based on sales from the team. I'd also earn a percentage of the investments in exchange for management. As he grew, so did I.

He liked this arrangement because it incentivized me to grow the team and operations. On top of this, I could sell houses and buy investments myself. I was now making good money almost purely in a Grinder fashion.

Want some help with negotiating? Read *Never Split the Difference* by Chris Voss.

Unexpected opportunities

But that wasn't all. Shortly after I quit, I realized how valuable my Cog experience actually was. My former company contacted me and requested I be available a certain number of hours per week at exactly twice my old rate. Easy and awesome. It wasn't results-based pay, so I limited it to 5 hours per week. They rarely used that much time.

In addition, one of my former co-workers left the company about 2 months earlier. He went Grinder big time. He started a major company with serious ambition and a lot of employees. My experience was valuable to him, and I was available at just the right time.

We initially worked out an hourly pay model, but I later renegotiated for a base with a results-based component. This is high-level work, helps keep my telecom skills sharp, pays well, and gives me a great opportunity to build my experience.

How I scaled it

These different types of work all lent to outsourcing. I've been able to pay assistants and leverage interns to scale my time. As I saw this happening, I found I didn't need to say "no" to opportunities. I just needed to take them and figure out how to manage them later.

All of this fell into place very quickly. And it was just the start. As I continued meeting people, my network began exploding. My results were noticed and requests for my services began compounding. I started posting better outcomes and building a reputation.

Ultimately, I began saying *no* to opportunities or providing massively high quotes. I had seen enough success helping people. It was time to focus on building my name, not others.

Grinder Summary

1. Most Grinders get their start by consulting.
2. Consultants generally make twice as much as their employee counterparts.
3. So, to get your first deals, leverage your network. Use your Mastermind Group and mentor.
4. Make money for results. Reduce their risk and expense of hiring you.
5. Once you get in with someone and start delivering results, it's time to re-evaluate your terms. Don't charge just an hourly rate.
6. Outsource repetitive or template-based work to assistants and interns. This is how you can scale.
7. Read *Never Split the Difference by Chris* Voss to learn how to negotiate from a top FBI negotiator.

Grinder Action: Your Consulting Sweet Spot

Going back to the text of this chapter, let's figure out the types of consulting you can provide by doing a skills inventory.

Get a sheet a paper and start making some lists:

1. What specific skills have you developed over time? Identify at least 20.
2. Which of those skills do you enjoy?
3. Which are you an ace at?

Once you have your list, think about which of those skills are not held or liked by people. Then, see if any of those skills are generally provided for a high fee. Do some internet searching to get an idea of pricing.

Go back and get your Mastermind Group's input. Talk to your mentor as well. Let them help you refine your ideas. See if they can introduce you to someone who might benefit from your services.

CHAPTER 19

Grinders Do Real Estate

Real estate investing meets the key Grinder money characteristics I've discussed so far.

Real estate is an awesome vehicle for both monthly income and long-term wealth. I mentioned it already, but the real-life Grinders I know have real estate investments. And many of them have A LOT of real estate. They don't necessarily pursue real estate as their primary income source, but all understand its true value.

> "Don't wait to buy real estate. Buy real estate and wait."
>
> ~ T Harv Eker, Secrets of the Millionaire Mind ~

What prevents Cogs from investing in real estate? Misconceptions. I'm not here to provide you with a full course on real estate investing, but I am here to help you understand its true power. I'd also like to shed light on those misconceptions, namely that you don't actually need as much money as you probably think to get started.

The Four Reasons Grinders Choose Real Estate

1. Cash Flow— Passive Monthly Income

Have I beaten these words into your head yet? I hope so. Investing in real estate gives you a consistent monthly income via collected rent. This is truly passive income (even the IRS agrees) that will grow regardless of the effort and time you put in.

Your cash flow is the amount you take home after expenses, such as the mortgage, property management fees, and other monthly expenses. It's delightful.

2. Mortgage Principle Pay Down— Net Worth Building

On top of the cash you receive every month, your property is also being paid down...every month. That's a double-edged advantage. You receive income, but in addition, your renter is *also* paying your mortgage for you.

I didn't internalize the power of this until I spent time with a real-estate-investing mentor. He is providing living space to people, which is his service. In exchange, he earns cash in his pocket every month. And those same tenants are also literally buying the properties for him.

Wouldn't you like someone to buy a house for you? That last sentence is worth reading again.

3. Appreciation— Net Worth Building

Looking at historical trends, real estate generally appreciates at consistently strong rates. When downturns in the real estate market occur, they are typically followed by corrections and the overall upward trend continues.

Real estate wealth building is a long-term game, so ups and downs don't matter. What matters is consistent appreciation, which holds very true with real estate.

After all, you can print more money, but you cannot print more land! You're dealing with a truly limited asset.

And while people will point out that stocks may grow faster than real estate, it is important to remember that stocks only change in terms of their appreciation. With real estate, you are gaining money in the other ways discussed here.

4. Tax Advantaged— Earnings Retention

Remember the math I showed earlier that illustrates how impactful it is to have lower taxes? Income from real estate holds multiple tax advantages: depreciation, passive income, interest, PMI write-offs, mileage, and expenses are all fair game (of course, talk to your tax accountant).

If you reduce your expense side, you have much more to keep for yourself and invest elsewhere.

The magic of investing in real estate

Not every real estate investor I know is wealthy, but every wealthy person I know is a real estate investor. As far as I know, I coined that saying, and I love it. It couldn't be truer.

Whether you buy property with 20% down or 0% down, there is some serious math set in motion that works tremendously in your favor.

Fundamentally, if done right, *someone else* (your tenant) buys a major asset for you. The bank floats you the cash and your tenants pay them back (and more).

How does real estate investing compare to stock investing?

Apart from the multiple ways you can make money from real estate investing, real estate has another key advantage: it is easy to valuate. I previously discussed the challenges in valuating stocks, but let me dive in a bit more here.

First, you generally have to buy stocks at face value. With real estate, you buy with a small percentage down, so your money is significantly leveraged. This multiplies your gains. You can't buy stocks with 20% down or less.

Next comes valuation. Analyzing complex, ever-changing companies and their associated stocks is *hard and futile*. Supposed experts cannot consistently figure this out, as illustrated by my previous reference to monkeys beating the pros year after year.

Real estate is much different. You can spend a couple of weekends looking at homes and very quickly get a great idea of how home values compare. Spend some time online and a good solid month checking out homes for sale on the weekends, and you will be a pro. You will understand exactly how to price homes in your area.

Home value consists of characteristics like neighborhoods, size, quantity of bedrooms and bathrooms, etc. What makes up the value of a home is vastly more basic than what makes up the value of a business. This means you will be able to identify good real estate deals more accurately than good stock deals.

Real estate is also *tangible*, which is a quality that is important to me. Stocks exist in cyberspace. Houses are physical things.

You can touch them. You can inspect their quality and see your investment whenever you want. I love this tangible aspect—it's great driving home and passing some investments on the way. It makes me feel proud of what I've accomplished and also proud that I'm able to provide a much-needed service. In my area, there is definitely a shortage of good rental homes.

Is real estate the most consistent path to becoming a self-made millionaire?

It may not be the fastest way to become a millionaire, but as far as I know, it is the *most consistent* way to do so. Since this book is about reducing your risk of leaving the grind behind, I value consistency over speed. Yes, the lottery is faster. Yes, launching a dotcom can be faster. But I want something that consistently wins.

Further, every—yes, every—millionaire I know has a real estate portfolio, and most started well before becoming millionaires.

Once you begin layering the cash flow, principle pay down, appreciation, and tax advantages, the money adds up quickly. And once you own several properties, you enjoy multiplication (aka my friend scalability).

In fact, Gary Keller has a terrific book called *The Millionaire Real Estate Investor*. In it, he outlines a simple plan to "Think $1 million, Buy $1 million, then Own $1 million" with real estate. It is a very concise and clear path to earning one million dollars. I haven't seen such a clear model anywhere else. And notice he starts with "thinking" first? People who know how to leave the grind behind know what is in Section 1 of this book.

> "Anyone can do it. Not everyone will. Will you?"
>
> ~ Gary Keller, The Millionaire Real Estate Investor ~

Do you have to be a landlord?

Absolutely not. And this is what removes you from the equation and makes it passive income. Great property managers and companies exist that charge a percentage of rent to handle the end-to-end management of your investment.

Most real estate owners will tell you that they actually make *more* money after hiring a property manager thanks to the professionalism and experience the manager brings. Property managers are in tune with the market, reduce your vacancy rates, and handle problem-tenants better.

Build property management into your analysis and let your money work for you.

Do you need a lot of money to invest in real estate?

Surprisingly, no. Many people I know invest very little of their own money. This was what allowed me to overcome my mental hurdle.

How could I ever have enough padding saved up to leave the grind behind if I had to dump all of my cash into buying real estate? Once I figured out how to get past this, I was able to establish cash flow to give me better padding than savings ever would. And I was able to do it without sacrificing my savings.

If you can find a deal at the right price, you can easily cover the cost of financing. And there are many ways to achieve 100% financing. You just need to research.

Plus, you don't need a $252,000 education or years to learn how. Real estate investing is built on consistent fundamentals, and they are not difficult. I've already explained why real estate is easy to valuate. You also need to understand how to properly finance it.

What you will learn is investing in real estate is a business, and you can get people to invest in your real estate business in exactly the same way they would invest in any other business of yours. This cost is built into your cash flow analysis, just like any business. Take the time to understand how to do this, and you'll remove money as an obstacle.

Can I really get a property for little or no money out of pocket?

The answer is yes. The long answer is more than can be offered in this book, but you will find *many* ways to achieve creative financing if you connect with the right education.

Ultimately, if you want to have the property entirely financed, you will need to build multiple sources of financing into your analysis. You may initially earn lower cash flow, but the right investment property will pay for the financing and more. The bottom line is don't let lack of cash hold you back. In truth, lack of education is holding you back.

I know people who purchase single-family homes with nothing down. I also know people who purchase multi-family homes (think small apartment complexes) with zero down. They quickly add six figures to their net worth and monthly cash flow that allows them to leave the grind behind.

Another situation you may be in is you have a lot saved but don't want to tie your savings up in real estate. You're about to quit your job so you want the padding. I can relate to this.

Search "creative financing" online. You can also email me at justin@grindbehindbook.com if you would like some recommendations on where to start.

What about the risks of real estate investing?

Have you heard of people losing massive amounts of money in real estate downturns? Horror story tenants? Houses sitting vacant for years?

Here's the thing. The owner probably didn't educate themselves on how to understand and buy cash flow. Even if the rental market in my area dropped by a massive 50%, I would still be making money. Others I know are even more protected. I am not worried about losing my cash flow at all, precisely because I did my research.

Second, people who lose in real estate sell when they should buy. Just like with the stock market, losses only count if you sell. When the market takes a massive dive, most people freak out and sell. Big mistake. You just locked in your losses. What do Grinders do? They *buy*. This is an opportunity to buy cheap. If the financial and real estate markets are crashing around you, you should see opportunities to pick up cheap stuff.

The value of the home only matters if you sell. When values drop, Cogs panic and sell. And who do they sell to? Grinders.

Lastly, don't take advice from accidental landlords. There are many people who fall into this category. Perhaps they inherited a home. Or perhaps they couldn't sell their house, but had to move, so they rented it out. Either way, they didn't specifically intend to have a real estate business. They were dropped in or stayed in for convenience.

Their experience with real estate will not match the experience of someone who has taken steps to educate themselves and purchase property as a business from the start.

There are of course many other operational risks to real estate investing, but they can be figured out and solved pretty easily. If you're ready to start a passive-income business, you just need to take some basic steps to educate yourself and add the right people to your network. It's a simple and highly lucrative game—don't be a Cog and miss out.

Grinder Summary

1. Real estate investing meets the key Grinder money characteristics.
2. You don't need as much money as you think to invest in real estate.
3. Real estate has four Grinder finance pillars:
    a. Cash Flow – Passive Monthly Income
    b. Mortgage Principle Pay Down – Net Worth Building
    c. Appreciation – Net Worth Building
    d. Tax Advantaged – Earnings Retention
4. Real estate math is magic. Between the bank and your tenants, someone else buys a property for you. And, they pay you for the privilege.

5. Real estate is better than stocks because it gives you more than just appreciation, is easier to valuate, and can be leveraged.

6. It may not be the fastest, but real estate is the most consistent path to being a self-made millionaire.

7. The risks of real estate investing are largely overblown and can be overcome with education.

8. Don't let lack of cash hold you back. The reality is lack of education is holding you back. Creative financing is what you need to learn about.

9. Read *The Millionaire Real Estate Investor* by Gary Keller to learn the game. This book provides a complete model for becoming a self-made millionaire through real estate. All you have to do is execute on it.

Grinder Action:
Real Estate Investing Preparation

There are a few simple steps you can take to massively improve your real estate investment understanding. Get them done.

1. Find someone you know who invests in real estate *and* is not an accidental investor. Take them out to lunch, give them a call, or whatever. Hear out their story, what they think of your market, and what recommendations they have for you to get started.

2. Unless you have enough money to quit your job and invest in real estate at the same time, research creative

finance for real estate investing. Warning: there are a lot of gurus out there in this space. Stick to well-known sources or email me at justin@grindbehindbook.com for recommendations.

3. Call a traditional lender—perhaps someone at your local bank—and see about getting pre-qualified for an investment loan. They will go over your credit, debt-to- income ratios, and a few other stats. This will give you an idea of where you stand. But don't limit yourself to traditional lending, otherwise you'll take longer to get started and scale more slowly.

CHAPTER 20

Make Money Online Within One Year

A major finding for me over the years is that making a lot of money doesn't need to be complex. While one person may start a company that has its own offices, a staff of 200, and many needy clients, another person may start a company that nets the same, grows the same, but is run simply out of their home.

In other words, earning potential isn't tied to complexity. You can build a strong, highly profitable company and keep things simple. It's eye opening to see someone making six figures selling sunglasses they never see or touch. They've figured out an effective middle-man strategy. They've figured out that by spending x dollars on advertising, they can earn y dollars in revenue.

Make no mistake, I'm not talking about a "get rich quick" scheme. Instead, it's a prescription to work smarter and harder than the next guy. It's a prescription to devote your time and energy into building a simple money system. The only "trick" is it must be done online, where—*you guessed it*—you can scale. Learn how to leverage the reach the Internet affords us all.

In order to effectively build an online money machine, you're going to need education, real-life practice, and connections. You need everything in this book.

Fortunately, you can get your hands dirty very easily. If you're sticking to the habits from Section 1, you're probably about to explode with energy. This is perfect. You can begin using your newfound energy and passion to start learning the ropes of making money online while also enriching the lives of others.

My background in making money online

A big portion of my income comes from online activities that I enjoy. That's exciting! This means I'm doing something I like, providing great value to others, making money, and setting myself up for ongoing streams of income that will require little effort from me in the future.

My corporate background included a lot of "go-to-market" work. This means I was involved in creating products and offers, and then having those products adopted. Additionally, I have solid experience in business development work. I made the most of my Cog time and it paid off.

Leveraging this experience, I've helped numerous websites develop, grow, and monetize. Some of these websites generate thousands of search visits each day. Others rely on paid traffic. Regardless, they sell product efficiently and are fun to operate.

To me, selling online is a game. It is full of stats and data, giving you instant feedback on actions you take. It is exhilarating and exciting to watch results unfold. And it is all immensely scalable! (Did I say that already?) This experience has translated directly to what I'll share here about making money online.

Why you should make money online

Even though the Internet is well-established, it is still in a "gold rush" state. It's expanding fast, yet is accessible to the little guys. Some basic reasons to get an online business started as soon as possible are:

- Starting a website takes very little money.
- You can work on it in the margins—you don't need to quit your day job yet.
- It no longer takes specialized knowledge. The tools are mature, simple, and accessible for most computer users.
- You can sell pretty much anything. You should be able to leverage your expertise and translate that into value you can offer others. Even if "everyone else" is already doing it, you can still bring in your own fresh view.
- Adding more to an existing market is not a bad thing. For example, you could say there are too many resources in the personal development space. But I go through about 2 books per month on this topic and am always seeking new information to keep myself motivated and sharp. I actually think there is a lack of information in this "crowded" space. Think of your niche the same way.

- If you're not yet sure what to sell, no problem. Of course, it's best to start with something to sell, but I didn't, and many others haven't either. Getting yourself out there has huge value in and of itself. You'll learn, build an audience, and prep yourself for that moment of inspiration.

- It is scalable. I'll probably say this yet again, so get used to it. Selling online to 1 person or 10,000 people requires little change in effort. But it sure will make a big change in your life.

Getting online fully fits into the principles of making money as described in this book. You could start by impacting only a handful of people but quickly be able to impact thousands or millions. I like that math.

The Plan to Make Money Online

"Content is king. Content is where I expect much of the real money will be made on the Internet, just as it was in broadcasting. ...the broad opportunities for most companies involve supplying information or entertainment. No company is too small to participate."

~Bill Gates~

I've learned there are 9 steps to getting started making money online. Of course, there are many different ways to go about this, but I'll focus on generating content—whether through writing, videos, or audio.

As you develop this content, you'll later use it to create your own products such as books, courses, software, or something else. This is content that you can ultimately sell.

You can make your entire living doing this. Or you can plan on this being a secondary stream of income.

Wait, is content really the best way to make money online?

No. The best way to make money online is to sell something that requires little manual effort to get out the door. The best way is to have a money tree that costs less to market and ship than the revenue it brings in. You can advertise and tie that expense directly to revenue. The model is simple: you pay $5 in advertising to make $10 in sales. You are printing money.

This is where you want to end up. You want to begin printing money. If you have a product to sell that meets a market demand, don't waste your time finishing this chapter. Go work with someone who can get you online quickly and can help you navigate the excellent world of online advertising.

But, if you don't have something ready to sell, finish reading this chapter. It will show you how to get the ball rolling.

Once you get yourself out there and start receiving exposure, you will be shocked by the amount you learn, the connections you make, and the ideas you generate. If you do what I recommend here, I expect you will have something outstanding to sell online within one year. And that means you'll be printing money before you know it.

Plus, getting your ideas online keeps life fresh and fun. It forces you to do something interesting. Since I can't say it better myself, check out Ben Franklin's take:

> "Either write something worth reading or do something worth writing."
>
> ~Benjamin Franklin~

So here are my nine steps to making money online.

1. Consult your life purpose and interests, to figure out your starting point

Go back to the work you've already done throughout this book. Think about something you like to write about or tell people about, something in which you have *reasonable* expertise and background.

Ensure that you truly enjoy the topic. Your passion will come across and help distinguish you from other experts and…most importantly…from people out to just make an easy buck.

People will latch on to your enthusiasm and gravitate toward you if you're genuine. There are a lot of sleazy gurus out there, but you can run circles around them with passion. Most customers see right through sleaze.

From this list, identify where you have some demonstrated real-world results. For example, if you'd like to write about exercise and weight loss, do you have your before-and-after numbers? Have you been able to repeat, maintain, and overcome? How many other people have you helped? What have their results been?

If you're at a loss for ideas, get going with your Mastermind Group! Never allow yourself to get stuck. That's what your group is there for. Your answer is out there—you just need the right minds working for you.

2. Determine which of your interests sells well online

Now start reviewing your topics. Is there an established market? Are other smaller players selling products and services that interest you? Are there a lot of books and programs to help people out?

It may sound a bit counter-intuitive to enter a market that is already big, but there are reasons this is the best option. Basically, it's a lot easier to jump into an existing market than to create your own.

What sounds easier to you: creating a new $1 million-dollar market from scratch or carving out 1% of an existing $100 million-dollar market?

Once you're in your market, you will naturally begin to diversify and find your own niche. Even if the market seems crowded, people will like variety and unique perspectives, which you can offer. And as you grow, you will learn how to make your offering unique and differently valuable.

Oftentimes, this inspiration comes from interacting with your audience and seeing what interests them. Big dogs get unseated constantly by up-and-comers they didn't see coming. There's no reason this can't be you.

As a final checkpoint, see if your topic has an established community, such as a forum or dedicated social system. It will be easier to bring attention to yourself if there are active communities, podcasts, and blogs about your topic.

While it might seem like competition, the reality is others creating content on your topic will be happy to interview you, feature you on their podcast, and more. People who have set themselves up in the cadence of doing weekly interviews are starving for guests and fresh viewpoints.

Getting yourself into a market that has such a community will fast-track your exposure and is a fundamental requirement.

3. Pick the topic you will use to make money online

Now that you've done research, it's time to decide. From your list of interests, rate them along these variables:

- Your level of passion and interest.
- Strength of your personal results, experience, and background.
- How strongly established the market is.
- The depth of community in the form of forums, podcasts, and blogs.

If you have a standout topic that scores well in all of these areas, you're on the right track.

4. Start your website—it's easy and accessible

Now it's time to commit. Get yourself a website! This is actually pretty simple, and you'll find the hardest part of this will be deciding on your website's name (see Step 5).

As you begin to build your website, you want to choose between a piecemeal approach and an "all-in-one" solution.

- If you want full control and flexibility, you'll do something like get hosting from GoDaddy, use WordPress for your content, layer in an email solution, a shopping cart, payment gateway, and more.
- On the other hand, you may look for something that provides an end-to-end solution. You may lose some flexibility, but the reduction in time-to-market and hassle may be well worth it.

A lot of this will depend on your skillsets, interests, and expertise too. You may enjoy tinkering and integrating web components, or you may not.

Do the research on your own—something fantastic may be available to shortcut your launch.

5. Choose your website's name wisely

This is probably the hardest part about starting to make money online, and it's a decision that will stick with you for quite some time.

Once you've signed up with a host, you'll be able to register your domain name. It should be simple and easy for people to remember, type, and read. It should contain some words relevant to the topic.

One great tool to help you out is "Google's Keyword Planner." In order to access it, you'll have to register your Gmail account with Google Adwords, but it's free and easy. Once you get there, choose the "multiply keywords to get new keyword ideas" option. There, you'll be able to enter a brainstorm of words and let Google kick you back some combination ideas. It will also give you data on usage and competition.

6. Set up your email list—your key to making money online

One of the most valuable things any business has is its database of customers and prospects. If you have something great, you need to tell people about it!

And if you're familiar with selling, people often don't care to buy on the first shot. Rather, they'll want to hear about it multiple times and grow convinced of its value. They need to "know" you and trust you. Customer and prospect lists provide the ability to reach, message, and nurture. In fact, lists are so important that businesses are often purchased because of them.

For this reason, I highly recommend starting off with the right email list solution. I made the mistake of going with a free one to start. The same is true of most of the people I have consulted.

Once you begin growing and making money, you will likely find that you need to switch from a free service to one with better features. This can be painful. Horribly painful.

Even the best email list services are cheap to start, and the cost will grow as you grow. Since this is perhaps the most valuable component, make the small investment here. If money is a concern, avoid eating out once per month, and you should have your cost covered.

So do yourself a favor and start with a professional email solution. If you spend your money anywhere, it should be here.

And this is where the rubber meets the road. If your website isn't selling something yet, your only goal should be building an email list. You want people signing up to be part of whatever it is you're doing. You will use analytics tools to set up "email opt-ins" as the website's goal, and every action will be measured against the success of this goal.

7. Start creating your unique, personalized, content *now*

While there is still a lot to learn, don't hesitate to start putting your energy to paper. Write your first posts. Don't worry about the thousands of details out there. There will be plenty of time to refine what you're doing, but every moment you don't create content is a moment you are falling behind.

Trust me: one year from now, you'll be happy you started today.

Ultimately this content you create can and should have massive potential for reuse. It can be repackaged into books, products, and other "for sale" items. But for now, it's a way for you to get yourself introduced and also build a reason for people to come to your site. You can also use it in the near future to refer people to great services that can earn you money.

One of the best resources for inspiring and guiding your approach to content marketing is the Content Marketing Institute (www.contentmarketinginstitute.com). They provide a wealth of research, inspiration, and guidance that you can use to progress your work over time. The founder also has written several excellent books, but you can start with *Epic Content Marketing* by Joe Pulizzi to get a flavor of their simple approach.

8. Think twice before selling other people's stuff

As soon as you start getting traffic, you'll become eager to make money. You'll notice other sites running advertisement and promoting other people's products. While this is not always a mistake, trying to make money too early this way will hurt you for these reasons:

- It detracts from your user experience.
- It pulls people away from your site–you want people on *your* site!
- It will likely earn you very, very small fees. Once you have high traffic, you should be able to earn from this type of advertising, but at the start, you're talking pennies.
- The largest problem is that it creates a mixed goal. Your site already has a goal: to get people to opt in. You're building a list to sell to (even if you're not yet ready to sell

something). These people will tell others about your site, join you on social media, and be your growth engine. If your site is selling advertisements and promoting other people's products, you have conflicting goals. Trust me, email lists full of people are a gold mine and will allow you to capitalize once your moment of inspiration comes. Don't conflict or confuse your audience by trying to monetize too early.

9. Promote, promote, promote

This is tough for a lot of people, but it's the most critical skill to learn and fear to overcome. Remember, leaving the grind behind is about marketing and sales. Well, here's your chance to prove you're a Grinder.

You must yell from the rooftop about every single thing you do online. Every post you make, every picture you post. Scream about it. If you love your content, someone else will too—but they have to know about it.

It's exceptionally easy to get a website up and running; the barriers to entry are few. This means you're entering a crowded space. Is that a reason to worry? No! But it does mean you have to do what others won't. That's what Grinders do. They do more than the next guy, and because of that, they win. To get what most people don't have, you have to do what most people won't.

Standing out online means relentless promotion. Adopt the motto, "If you don't know my name, that's my fault."

Everyone should know your name. They should see you everywhere.

Full out attack via social media, email, forums, and more is required. Promoting yourself is an art you'll probably mess up for a while. But ultimately, if you're offering valuable information and content you love, I guarantee people will be happy you are sharing and also be happy to follow.

And guess what? Once you master promotion, you master selling. This means you can sell your products and services. It means you can sell other people's products and services. This makes you massively valuable. You can add to a business' bottom line. That's a big deal.

What You Really Get from this Work

If you have become excited about getting the most from life and making money in a way you are passionate about, you owe it to yourself to hop on this modern-day gold rush. Hopefully this portion of the chapter has given you a primer. There's much more to learn, but don't over-complicate things…just get going.

You have so much to gain and, really, just a very small amount of money and time to lose. The actions in this chapter are completely in sync with the principles described throughout this book. They are low risk, low cost, have massive potential, and can be done as you transition from your Cog job.

Here are some of the key fringe benefits that will come along with it:

1. You will make unexpected connections, which will grow your vital network, give you new ideas, and open you to

new possibilities. Some of my best connections resulted from pushing content online.

2. You will learn how to sell to people and grow businesses.

3. You will generate content that will become something worth packaging and selling some day.

4. You will develop new skillsets and marketable capabilities.

5. Skills that you can sell via consulting as you leave the grind behind.

6. Start now and you can be somewhere completely different this time next year.

Grinder
Summary

1. Think simple. You can start a business that nets you six figures with 0 employees. You could also start a business that nets you six figures but needs 200 employees. Which is better?

2. Devote your time and energy to finding and building a simple money machine.

3. This is not a "get rich quick" prescription. Instead, it's a prescription to work smarter and harder than the next guy.

4. You can start an online money machine cheaply and easily.

5. If you have an idea and something to sell, get started and pay someone to get you up and running quickly.

6. If you don't yet have an idea, get started on creating content.

7. If you get yourself online now, you will thank yourself in a year. You will have highly valuable skills, a much bigger and more diverse network, and you will have something to sell.

Grinder Action: Make Your Online Plan

Go through the steps in the "The Plan to Make Money Online" portion of this chapter and pick something you want to create content on. There are simple content platforms for blogs, video, and audio. Whatever it is, pick something and get started.

Try to brainstorm at least 10 solid options. I suggest you regularly brainstorm more options than you think you need. It will force you to dig a bit and it will also reduce your risk. If you only have one item and it doesn't pan out, you'll get discouraged and stop. Or, if you present that one idea to people and they shoot it down, you may never start.

By having a list of 10 solid options, you're saying, "I'm doing this, and here are 10 ways I'm thinking of going about it." People will help you choose the best option from the list; you're more likely to get something rolling; and you also have some fallback if it doesn't work. Your Mastermind Group is there to provide brainstormed input and analysis for your list, so make sure to leverage it.

SECTION 3

Summary

Money is the reason most of us are Cogs. Money is the reason we go to work for someone else every day. We need it to pay for our house, our food, and our lifestyle. We need it to support ourselves and our family. But if this is your relationship with money, you're working for it rather than making it work for you.

Section 3 is all about getting money to work for you. To do this, you have a lot of conditioning to undo and a lot of new education ahead. If you're going to pack all of this in, you need to start by being ruthless with your time. Clear the waste from your life. Focus your energy.

Challenge your notions of the best ways to make money. Build the skills that make real money, including execution, sales, and marketing. Use them to create your own money machine. Let the words passive and scalable work wonders for you.

As with each section, I have something to help you stay focused. Go to **grindbehindbook.com/tools**. Print out the weekly worksheet. It will keep you on track and accountable.

And most importantly…get going. Hopefully there were several "aha" ideas in this section that got you thinking or piqued your interest. And now that you've read this whole book, you have the resources to leave the grind behind. It's time to change your life. Make yourself proud.

FINAL THOUGHTS

The Grinder's Graduation

Next Steps

I want to thank you from the bottom of my heart for reading. Leaving the grind behind has been an absolutely liberating journey for me. My life has improved so much that I've vowed never go back to being a Cog. Writing this book cements that vow.

Will you take a similar vow? Vow to go forward and enjoy a life designed by you and no one else. Enjoy it so substantially that your energy overflows and improves the lives of those around you.

To keep your momentum blasting, head to:

GrindBehindBook.com/tools

There, you'll find great **free bonuses** including:

- 100 Tips to Quit Your Job this Year
- The Grinder Master's Course
- All the worksheets and tools from this book

Here's where else to find me:

- justin@grindbehindbook.com
- facebook.com/grindbehind
- twitter.com/grindbehind

About the Author

Justin Gesso holds an MBA and had a good run in corporate America. He was able to make the leap to working on multi-million-dollar startups, while also pursuing numerous other exciting projects and investments.

Along with solid achievements in the professional arena, Justin has also been able to maintain a personal life rich in family, health, and community.

Justin has been practicing and refining the principles you'll see in this book for over a decade. These practices are the result of reading hundreds of books and having some of the best professional and personal coaches in the world.

Within just one-and-a-half years of quitting his day job, Justin was able to double his six-figure income. Within two years, he doubled his net worth. He was also able to rapidly build an $800,000 real estate portfolio. And that all is just a start.

Justin has realized repeated success in multiple business ventures, defying the startup failure rate. As a result, he has been featured in numerous publications and broadcasts, including Fox, ABC, CBS News, NBC, The Huffington Post, and many more.

And of course, none of this would be possible on the *standard* path. In order to achieve these goals, Justin had to leave the grind behind.

Justin is committed to enabling millions of others to leave their job, achieve their dreams, and live a life they design.

Acknowledgements

First and foremost, I want to acknowledge and thank my beautiful wife. Once upon a time, my secure job provided us with a handsome salary, delightful benefits, and a very comfortable lifestyle. Yet she didn't bat an eye when I said, "I want to quit and do something better." Her unwavering belief and support made the first step of this journey and more possible.

I want to offer my unconditional thanks to my son, who inspires me to do my best and causes me to see the world from unique perspectives.

My parents have believed in me since day one. They pushed me to do my best and take a holistic view on life. Their positive influence continues to be invaluable and cherished.

This book's editor, Greg Helmerick, has helped me take fluttering ideas and turn them in to the untangled words you find here. He has provided loyal friendship along the way too.

Next, I want to recognize key mentors. Thanks to Jim Steele for being my first official mentor and kicking me off the slow path. Mark Ferguson pushed me over the edge by showing what's possible. Ashok Reddy continues to impress the value of big vision and exceptional execution. And for providing a shining example of brotherly love and selfless behavior, Jerry Hager, I thank you.

Last, to my friends, mentors, mastermind members, and brothers: you know this path wouldn't have been possible without you. Thank you all.

One Last Thing

Allow me to ask you a favor. If you enjoyed this book and feel your life has improved as a result…

Give a copy of *Leave the Grind Behind* to a friend or family member.

Help from people like you is how I can achieve my ambitious goal of improving the lives of *millions*. I hope you set a similar goal.

Best regards and thank you,

Justin Gesso

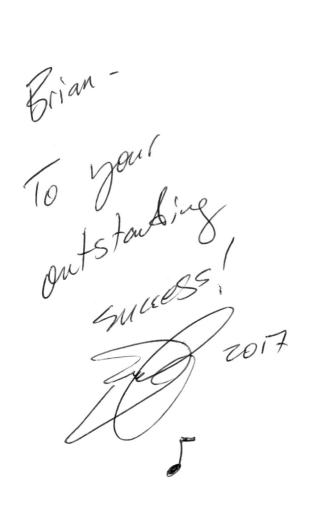

Brian –

To your outstanding success!

2017

45899816R00184

Made in the USA
Middletown, DE
16 July 2017